LOVE

The Grace of
LOVE

Pastor William R. Grimbol

ALPHA

A Pearson Education Company

This book is dedicated to Bob Jaklich Jr. My best man. My friend. My son. My father. My student. My mentor. In all things, we have built a relationship rooted in unconditional love. It has been an experience of pure Grace.

(I must have played you in a thousand one-on-one games of basketball. I never won. Not even once. I have forgiven you ... but you should repent a bit longer, just to be safe.)

International Standard Book Number: 0-02-864430-1
Library of Congress Catalog Card Number: 2002111656
04 03 02   8 7 6 5 4 3 2 1
Interpretation of the printing code: The rightmost number of the first series of numbers is the year of the book's printing; the rightmost number of the second series of numbers is the number of the book's printing. For example, a printing code of 02-1 shows that the first printing occurred in 2002.
Printed in the United States of America

For marketing and publicity, please call: 317-581-3722
The publisher offers discounts on this book when ordered in quantity for bulk purchases and special sales.
For sales within the United States, please contact: Corporate and Government Sales, 1-800-382-3419 or corpsales@pearsontechgroup.com
Outside the United States, please contact: International Sales, 317-581-3793 or international@pearsontechgroup.com

Contents

Introduction

I recently watched a bunch of old television shows. We just got cable, and I love having *Nick at Night.* I spent a whole evening watching *Love Boat; Love, American Style; The Newlywed Game;* and *The Dating Game.* Man, those were some silly shows. Watching them was a revelation. Those shows made love look so easy, like a hobby, an amusement, a pleasant diversion.

I know what you are thinking: I must have known these shows were meant just for fun. Yes, I did know that. However, the fact remains that these were the shows that helped educate me on love. I was raised on a steady diet of seeing love as something I could learn in an afternoon. I grew up thinking love was a snap, just a trivial pursuit.

My family was also not much help. I was loved to the point of worship and adoration. This made me unable to receive criticism or genuinely respect difference. My parents' marriage was neither romantic nor lusty. They functioned like quarreling siblings. Though there was a ton of love in my house, it was splattered everywhere. Yes, we all got hit. We even got doused at times. But I failed to distinguish any purposeful pattern, just a squirt here and a splash there, a mess of love, a lovely mess.

In my senior year of college, I read a remarkable book by Erich Fromm called *The Art of Loving*. I was so moved by his insights. Love was an art, he said. It required practice and discipline. There were skills we needed to know, rules and roles and rituals. Loving was work, good work, meaningful work, satisfying work, even joyful work. But for the first time in my life, I found out that love required genuine effort.

In Seminary, I studied the life of Jesus Christ as well as explored many other religions. Each was focused on a God whose essence was love. Each spoke of love that was unconditional. There were no hooks, no games, no paybacks, just love for the sake of love. This love was spoken of as grace. I came to believe that Jesus was the event of grace. His love was extravagant, reckless, even extreme. He went so far as to love enemies and outcasts.

In my ministry, I have continued my education in love. I have witnessed acts of love so gracious and generous I have been moved to tears. I have seen the damage done by the absence of love, which also has made me weep. I have seen firsthand love's power to heal. I have watched couples tear apart the fabric of their family in search of their one true love. I have listened to endless stories of lost loves. I have come to see that we are full of love yet seldom know when or where or how to express it.

I see this book as a sacred opportunity. It is my chance to share what I know about love, to offer my small portion of wisdom. I do so with confidence. Why? Because there is so little written about love that is honest. Honest love is rooted in the reality of daily living. Honest love deals with ordinary lives and average friendships and families, not like marriages found on *Jerry Springer*. We should be willing to take the risks that challenge us to be better and smarter in our loving. I fully intend to speak with candor and to call us to higher ground.

I have faith that this book will be of help to you. Even if it covers old ground, it will remind you of some favorite spots along the way. Hopefully, it will lift up some new insights for you or at least make you see some aspects of loving in a new light. No matter what, I think you will know I offer it in the spirit of love, not as a simple solution, not as some gimmick or bag of tricks, and definitely not as a how-to book. This book is solely meant as a frank and spiritual discussion of life's most vital topic—*love*.

Acknowledgments

Words. They can be so powerful. They have the capacity to heal and offer hope. They can make or break a relationship. They can start a war, or end one.

Writing is creating with words. At times, the writing becomes too personal, obsessive, cluttered with emotion and attitude and the human desire to explain the world and life. The job of an editor is to keep the writer, or at least this one, on task and target, to narrow my scope, but to free my words to say even more than I had hoped.

Working with an editor is a spiritual event. It is the placing of one's soul in another's hands. Nancy Lewis has been my soul mate on these three books. Her work has been amazing. She has a great eye. She can see what I am trying to say. She has an ear for how to say it best. She has infused my writing with clarity and beauty. She has been a gift.

I also wish to thank Christy Wagner and all other editors who have helped give spiritual shape to this book, and whose editing skills are evident on every page. Each has left the tracings of their talent. Good writing is a group effort.

I also wish to thank Randy Ladenheim-Gil. We have never met, and yet I would trust her with just about everything. In working on bringing these projects to fruition, I have come to know that Randy is a woman of significant intelligence, competence galore, and a remarkable ability to inspire. My thanks to Randy. Let's do lunch.

Can We Talk?

Words can sometimes, in moments of grace,
attain the qualities of deeds.
—*Elie Wiesel*

Joan Rivers is a sassy and brassy comedienne whose signature line is "Can we talk?" after which she goes on to spout her humor on a wide range of topics. Basically, she will talk about anything, especially those subjects most of us choose to avoid.

If I were to seriously answer her not-so-serious question, it would be a resounding "NO!" No, we can't talk. We don't seem to know *how* to talk. We can't find the time to talk. We don't want to get too personal, so we keep most of who we are a secret. We won't talk about anything that might produce conflict or a difference of opinion, so we don't talk about anything that matters. We are uncomfortable speaking spiritually, so we seldom address the subjects of faith, hope, or love.

It is not that we don't talk. We talk all the time. Our lives are full of chatter. Our television screens are dominated by talk shows. We have free speech, but, unfortunately, that is what much of it is worth—talking about nothing, killing time with chit-chat, gossiping and complaining, filling the air with useless information, conversation that feels rehearsed or forced, and banal banter.

What is missing is good conversation, meaningful talks, delving deep into a subject. We must choose our words with care, mean what we say and say what we mean, and have something of value to offer. We need to speak on topics we know something about, offer an opinion as just that—an opinion, show some humility and some respect for language and the listener. We need to remember to approach communication as an art.

To become a master in the art of relationship communication, we must be fluent in the language of love. We need to express our love in thought, word, and deed. Our love should not have to be intuited, neither should it require interpretation. Our love must be made plain … clear … obvious. Speaking our love might not be the sole priority of communication, but it is way ahead of whatever comes in second.

As a minister, a major aspect of my job is to enable love. I preach on it. I teach about it. Most of my counseling is directly related to it. The whole ministry and message of Jesus Christ is grounded in love. Love is his top priority. He asks us to aim our lives at love. It is impossible to claim a faith in Jesus and not be equally committed to loving.

No matter what your faith may be, I doubt it has overlooked the central importance of love and loving. When we boil life down to its essence, we are left with matters of the heart—in particular, love. Love is, indeed, *the* answer. It is the heart's desire, our deepest longing, the call of God. If we are addressing the issue of having a happy and healthy life, we are speaking about love.

Opening Up

If we want someone to love us, we need to open ourselves to that person. We need to let them know what we think, what we feel, and what we believe. We must let them get past our image. We must let them inside, to our innards, to our emotional and spiritual side. The chief risk of loving is revelation. We are letting our true selves be seen. We are stripping away all the camouflage, peeling off the masks, and removing the makeup.

The same holds true if we are trying to love someone. We must work at getting to know that person, at knowing her deepest thoughts, at letting her tears roll down our cheeks, at searching her soul. We must display interest. We must take time to get to know her. We must hold what we know as a cherished object. We must prove ourselves trustworthy.

We live in a culture that encourages us to be covered up and shut down. In America, image is everything. It is as if we were all for sale. We have to look right. We have to sound right. We have to act right. We have to be with the right people. The problem is that all this "rightness" may be all wrong for us. Our real self gets lost. Our soul gets sold to the highest bidder. We wind up feeling empty, lonely, and lost.

In 25 years of ministry, I have counseled hundreds of folks. I long ago realized that many people come for counseling only because they need to have an honest conversation. They need to open up. They need to let their true feelings show. They need to get something off their chest. They need to be known. They want to find out if their real self is loveable.

If the truth be known, the real self is all that is loveable. We can't love an image. We can't love a lifestyle.

We can't love a clique or class. We can love somebody. We can love them if we know them, inside out, if we have touched their heart, if we have gotten inside their soul. True love is dependent on knowing the true self.

Express Your Self

I often hear men say, "Oh, I don't have to say it. She knows what I feel." Wrong! How stupid! If you feel it, say it. Why leave someone wondering? Why make them guess? Can we imagine Jesus saying "Well, you know how I feel." We have mouths that are meant to be used, not necessarily to say everything we think or to share each emotion, but, yes, to speak about what matters most to us.

When working with couples, I am aghast at how little and how seldom they talk. Talking is limited to messages over morning coffee, a "How was your day?" at dinner, "Will we or won't we have sex tonight?" "What channel do you want?" "What are you reading?" and several statements that begin, "Don't forget to …" or "We need to talk about …." The talking, of course, never happens.

Part of the problem is that we are too busy. It is hard to find the time for a good conversation. Another problem is that we are too tired. A good conversation takes energy. Still another problem is finding a place where it is safe to talk. A good conversation does require privacy and a lack of interruption. There is also the problem of having lost the habit and forgotten how. For many of us, it has been so long since we *really* talked, we are not sure if we even remember how to.

There is also one other problem: fear of conflict. Many people don't talk because of the sense that touching upon sensitive issues or important topics will lead to an argument. Many relationships wither and rot from conflict avoidance. They just hang there on the vine, dead. They have avoided conflict and lost life all at the same time.

I know. Many of you are saying "Well, that is true. I can't find the time or place or energy to have a good conversation, and I don't even know if we can do it. Plus, every time we try, we start fighting." The problems I have presented are real. Think of it this way: If we don't deal with those problems, our relationships will eventually die. Even if we are together, the love will have stopped beating.

If a doctor tells us that our heart requires an hour of daily exercise or we may have cardiac arrest, most of us will get busy walking, biking, swimming, or doing something. The same is true of our spiritual heart. It also needs exercise. It needs good conversation. It needs to be known, understood, loved. Isn't it time to take care of our souls? It is time to talk!

Tell It Like It Is

Earlier in my career, I shared ministry with a man who prided himself on being honest—brutally honest. He was forever pointing out the flaw in the plan or the individual. We spent endless hours focusing on our flops. Each mistake was magnified for inspection. Our whole ministry was conducted in an atmosphere of inspection. The whole staff knew we were under heavy surveillance.

I am older now and a bit wiser. I certainly know more about ministers and ministry. I now know that my colleague back then was not being brutally honest. He was being in control. He was letting us know who was in charge. He was making it clear, on a daily basis, who was head of staff. His honesty was an excuse to declare power and position. It was often mean-spirited, and never once was his honesty positive, let alone loving.

Good conversation must be honest. Honesty must also be tempered with timing and tenderness. There are times to speak our minds, and there are times that are all wrong. There are words that need to be heard, and there are words that would bury someone in pain. Our words must always demonstrate concern, compassion, and care. They should not be unleashed as a weapon. They need to be presented in a positive, productive, and purposeful manner.

We can hear criticism if it is from someone we know cares about us. We can hear anger if we know it is not meant to punish or inflict harm. We can handle conflict if we know the relationship is still committed to change and growth. A strong relationship is a safe context for most any dialog. The safety is the result of having consistently expressed love, respect, and trust.

Talk is not cheap. What we say matters. It counts to those we love. We must choose our words carefully. We must speak with tender honesty. We must risk addressing tough topics. We must do so in an environment of safety and security. We must declare our commitment and make clear our vows. Our love must be guaranteed.

We all desire open and honest relationships. We yearn to be understood. We long to be fully known. Talking is the doorway to deeply loving relationships. Even in our relationship with God, prayer—spiritual talking—is our lifeline. Without talking, a relationship will falter, and the love will fade.

Is there anything better or more healing and cleansing than having had a really good talk with someone we love?

The Questions

What do I need to talk about? What do I need to get off my chest? With whom do I long to share my truest self? What is keeping me from doing so? What am I afraid to share with those I love?

The Prayer

O God, can we talk? Can I admit to you how much I have to say? How much I long to share my soul with someone? How passionately I desire for understanding? O God, let me trust that you know me, fully, honestly, and wholly. May I know the grace of that knowledge. Amen.

Listen Up

*The greatest gift you can give another is the
purity of your attention.*
—Richard Moss, M.D.

When you lose a mate, you always have regrets—things
you wish you had said or done differently … or not at
all, things you wish you had remembered to do more
often. You think about all kinds of little and big things
for which you wish you had a second chance. It is so
hard to accept that you have used all your chances, that
all your opportunities are over.

I have one major regret, which might sound strange
to some: I wish I had been a better listener. I can't count
how many times my wife Christine, who died unexpect-
edly two years ago, said to me, "Would you please listen? Your mind is all over the place!" It was true. My
mind was often scattered, a mess. My listening was dis-
tracted. I failed to offer Christine my undivided attention. Far too often I heard her through a din of daily
worries and concerns.

I hate to admit it, but when she told me I was a lousy listener, I got defensive. How ironic—I would not hear that she was not being heard. She was right. I often failed Christine as a listener. I know that now. Grief is a powerful teacher. My regrets are just as powerful. I only wish I could have even one more conversation with Christine. I long to hear her voice. I could and would listen to her for hours.

Speaking from experience, I encourage all of you to take seriously your responsibility as a listener. Those we love deserve to be heard. Each and every word is more precious than you know. Every conversation is a sacred sharing of souls. There will come a time when your memory will clutch for the sound of a voice or the remembrance of a morning chat over coffee. Trust me, listening matters.

All Ears

There are times when I am a good listener. In counseling, for example, I try my best to be all ears, to absorb every word being spoken. I also try to listen to the silences, the sighs, the slips of the tongue, the moments of hesitation. I even listen to the footsteps coming into the office as well as when they leave. A knock on a door can also be revealing.

I think of counseling as an opportunity to love someone. I mean it. If someone comes to my office and serves me their heart on a silver platter, the least I can offer in return is my love.

Love is all ears. Love cares about what the beloved has to say. Love wants to know and be known, to understand and be understood, to show respect and be respected. Love is focused. It pays attention. It notices every little thing. Love is a good listener.

Paying Attention

It's amazing how easy it is to tell if someone is really listening and how fast we know if we are being dismissed or missed altogether. The roaming eyes. The fidgeting. The lack of interest. The monotone speech. The memorized lines. "We really need to get together some time." "I was just thinking about you." "I will be sure to call." Yech. We all know when someone has moved onto the next event or person before a supposed conversation is complete. It is a lousy feeling, as if you do not matter. Or, worse yet, as if you aren't even there.

In fairness, someone who genuinely loves us, can, at times, be preoccupied. His mind can be off and running in another direction. We can forgive someone for failing to pay attention, but it becomes harder if that failure keeps on repeating itself. A lack of attention speaks a lack of love. It also shows zero respect. It erodes confidence and trust.

Paying attention is a choice. Try it. Make the decision to give someone your undivided attention and your full focus. Listen with your heart and mind. Notice the details. Show empathy. Feel what they feel. Crawl into their space. Live in their shoes and soul. It is an extraordinary experience. It is hard not to love someone once you have gone inside.

To offer your full attention is a wonderful gift. It is a true expression of love. It speaks of a deep caring, a devotion, a commitment. It displays a respect. It lets someone know how much he matters to you, how crucial his words are, how treasured his thoughts and feelings are, and how safe his soul is in your hands. Paying attention coats a relationship in a layer of grace. It keeps it safe and pure.

Giving Voice

One of the greatest gifts of life is the chance to give voice to our wishes and dreams, our wants and needs, our fears and worries, our beliefs and ideas, our hopes and visions. Language is a defining characteristic of humanity; it unites and divides us. The language of love says it all. God is often called the Word. Amazing grace is named a sweet sound.

Giving voice is sacred. Our words can be eternal, holy. Our words can transform a day, a soul, a world. Language can close or open doors and make us feel at home or alienated. Speaking is the means by which we build friendships. Conversation is the framework of marriage and family. Chatter is the merry sound of neighbors. Praying is how we call upon God.

When someone gives voice to a feeling, thought, wish, dream, or idea, we have a sacred responsibility to listen. We must pay attention—close attention. We must focus. Giving voice is the opposite of making noise. Making noise is spewing words to fill time and space. Giving voice is offering words as if they were our children, cherished and adored.

When we give voice in prayer to our longings and hopes, we can be assured we have God's full attention. We are called by God to offer the same to those we claim to love. We are even asked to offer such faithful focus to strangers. Listening is what God does. It is who God is. Silence is simply God listening—all ears.

Listening is the foundation upon which true love is built. Love listens with the heart. Love fully absorbs the message and the meaning. Love consumes each word and digests it. It is fueled by it. It is energized by it. Love is an active listener, fully engaged, fully present.

The Questions
Am I a good listener? Do I offer those I love my full attention? Do I notice details? Do I give voice to my truest self? Do I give honor to those who give voice to their truest selves? Do I listen to God? Do I hear God's silence speak my name?

The Prayer
O God, I give thanks for your listening. You listen to me at all times and in all places. Your silence speaks my name. Your silence informs me of your presence. Your silence shouts of your love for me. May I listen to this silence. May I give voice to the gift that is your gracious ear. Amen.

Considerable Consideration

Feelings are everywhere—be gentle.
—J. Masai

I was born and raised in Racine, Wisconsin. My college years were spent at St. Olaf College in Northfield, Minnesota. At heart, I am a Midwesterner.

I recently returned to the area for a visit. I spent a long weekend at the St. James Hotel in Red Wing, Minnesota. I visited several of my favorite Minnesota towns: Winona, Wabasha, and Lake City, like Red Wing, all towns nestled along the banks of the Mississippi River. Of course, I also returned to Northfield for a nostalgic visit to my alma mater.

It was a truly wonderful visit. I haunted several of my favorite restaurants and shops. I walked familiar streets. I let the memories gently wash over me. The entire time I was aware of how good it felt to be in the Midwest. "What is it about the Midwest?" I wondered out loud.

Then it struck me. It is the kindness and graciousness of the people. Everywhere I went, the people were so welcoming. They moved slowly. They talked slow. They had time to listen. They were so considerate. Yes, this stretch along the mighty Mississippi is physically gorgeous, but it is the beauty of the people that is most impressive. What a joy it is to deal with people wearing a smile.

Midwesterners. Minnesotans. I am not sure who or what created this atmosphere of consideration, but I sure enjoyed experiencing it again. It felt good to order a meal from someone who seemed to care that everything was prepared just right. It felt good to shop at a store where the interest was not only in the sale. And having my windows cleaned at a full-service gas station was worthy of jubilation.

Everywhere I went, folks said "Hi." Conversations were as easy to start as a brush fire in August. Many people I met asked where I lived. I told them, "the Hamptons." Many had heard of it. Many thought it would be really something to visit the lovely, affluent villages that hug the Atlantic coastline at the end of Long Island. I thought to myself, "The Hamptons could take a course in civility and considerate behavior from these good folks."

Being considerate. It's so simple yet so important. Showing interest, showing you care, paying respect, treating someone as if he matters—this is basic human kindness. Cordiality, civility, speaking in a manner that invites a response, listening, hearing, being fully present, being available, being patient, being helpful—in the Midwest, it seems most folks have been trained in the art of being a good host.

Judges and Juries

I hate to dwell on the media, television in particular, but the fact is, it does reveal the state of our cultural soul. At present there are six shows on television featuring judges, *Judge Judy* being the most popular. Each judge issues justice swiftly, and most of the time with scorn. The more sarcastic the sentence, the higher-rated the show. Judgementalism has gone mainstream—it is back in fashion.

I have also tuned in to watch several of the television evangelists. They bang their Bibles and condemn gays, feminists, liberals, the ACLU, and, of course, Bill and Hillary. The Jesus they preach is white, American, Southern, conservative, rich, and Republican. America is the new Promised Land. Americans are the new Chosen

People. If you are not born again, if you have not been saved, these preachers promise a place has been saved for you in hell.

As a Christian, I find it comforting that Jesus reserved his wrath for the Pharisees and scribes—the religious elite of his time. Jesus called them hypocrites, white-washed tombs. He said that they looked all clean and shiny on the outside, but inside were full of a dead man's bones. He said they talked a good line about love and justice, but they lived with hate in their hearts.

Jesus condemned being judgmental. He told people to take the log out of their own eye before they pointed out the speck in their neighbor's. Jesus was furious when people of faith saw fit to condemn others. He asked his followers to withhold judgment and to never see them-selves as someone's jury.

It is impossible to love and to judge someone at the same time. It is equally impossible to feel love when we are being judged. Judging literally kills the spirit of love.

Showing Tolerance

I am not sure when it happened, and I do not know why it happened, but somehow, some way, *tolerance* became a bad word. I guess the notion now is that tolerance means anything goes. Tolerance came to be seen as a lack of boundaries or borders, an inability to draw a bottom line, a refusal to say no. To be tolerant was to be a pushover, a chump, a person with a limp spine.

I heartily disagree. Tolerance is giving someone the benefit of the doubt. It is giving a person a chance and, yes, maybe a second or third chance. It is not only withholding judgment, it is also offering encouragement. It is showing someone patience, kindness, and respect. It is treating someone as we would like to be treated.

Tolerance is the essence of civility. Civility shows respect for difference. Civility celebrates diversity. Civility looks for the best in others. Civility has a positive attitude. Civility does not critique or judge. Civility provides a safe context in which communication can take place. Civility is the soil in which the seed of love can be planted.

Being considerate is caring. It is caring about what someone feels and how he is doing. It is showing him respect, even when he may have done nothing to warrant it. Consideration is meeting someone halfway. It is reaching out to others. It is seeking to bring out the best in the people we meet.

Communication grounded in consideration will tend to be more open and honest and less judgmental. It will avoid competing and comparing, will not hit below the belt, and will not look for a weak spot. Consideration keeps the communication clean, unsoiled by our need to be right, unstained by the human tendency to turn discussions into debates. Consideration is a strong foreshadowing of someone who can be trusted.

The Questions
Am I a considerate person? Am I treated with consideration for what I think and feel and believe? What does it mean to me to be considerate? Who treats me with the greatest consideration? When and where and how am I most judgmental? Why is tenderness so vital to a loving relationship?

The Prayer
O God, let me show I care. Make me considerate of the feelings of others. Let me offer my interest and respect. Let me make it known that I want to be there, that I hope I can be a friend. Amen.

A Compromising Situation

Compromise makes a good umbrella,
but a poor roof.
—*James Russell Lowell*

I have served a total of five years on the Sag Harbor School Board. It has been a test of patience and endurance. At times I have thought of writing a book called *Board to Tears,* describing the odyssey. Being a member of a school board is some of the most emotionally draining work I have ever done.

It is odd. I like my fellow board members. I have worked with two fine superintendents. Our principals are outstanding. The other administrators are competence plus. We have a majority of superb, hard-working, loving teachers. The kids are great. The parents are tough, but, hey, it's their kids they are fighting for. The taxpayers are fair. What is it that makes it so damn difficult?

I have come to the conclusion that it is the lost art of compromise. The Board, the administrators, the teachers, the parents, the kids, the taxpayers—each sees himself as a faction. Each comes to the educational process on the defense or, worse yet, on the offense. Each is territorial. At times, one might have an ax to grind. Many decisions, especially the financial ones, become highly personalized. People feel used or assumed. There is bitterness. Each sees the other as the other side.

Every year we kick off the start of school by claiming that we are all in it together. We celebrate that it does take a whole village to raise a child. But when the issue is tenure, a contract, discipline, or a bond vote, folks tend to retreat to their corners—their constituency. By the end of the school year, factions are frequently feuding, not speaking at all, or treating one another with polite contempt. Issues of trust and respect are hotly debated. There are questions of conspiracy, secrecy, or a lack of honesty. Communication has broken down. What is left is gossip, innuendo, and sound bytes.

Compromise is built on trust. It is only possible if all sides respect one another. It is most successful if all sides believe they are fundamentally on the same side. Compromise demonstrates a belief that all parties are good people. Honesty is accepted as a given. Difference is both acknowledged and affirmed. Compromise is not seen as giving in or giving up. It is simply the process of determining what is in the best interest of *everyone.*

The Role of Respect

Think of someone for whom you have great respect. Imagine you must make a decision with that person. What assumptions would you make about the process of working as a team? First and foremost, you would assume that nothing would be said or done that was meant to do you harm. You would assume that your best interests would be protected, your wishes honored, your needs met, and your concerns addressed. You would approach the decision-making process with confidence and trust.

Respect is the key ingredient in compromise. Far too many relationships fail at compromise due to a lack of respect. If we do not feel that our intelligence, feelings, or beliefs are respected, or if we feel that we are not thought of as a true equal, it will be hard to find the common ground necessary for compromise. It may be hard to detect or admit this lack of respect. Many relationships have never acknowledged the inequity they have allowed to dictate the terms of their alliance.

Respect cannot always be earned. At times it must be assumed. This is never easy. It helps if there is a history of trustworthy behavior or a record of respect. Either way, we need to put our best foot forward. We need to offer respect as a means of negotiating. If we are proven wrong, so be it. Then we learn. I do think it is wise to come to the bargaining table, be it in a boardroom or kitchen, with a positive and hopeful attitude.

Respect enhances communication. It encourages risk-taking. It enables the swapping of souls. When problems arise, which they always do, the parties involved can move quickly and effortlessly toward compromise. Respect is the catalyst for compromise. Compromise is required in every strong and durable relationship. Love cannot exist over time without exercising the art of compromise.

Mutual Gains

The best experience I've had being on the Sag Harbor School Board was, of all things, a contract negotiation. Our superintendent recommended we use a system called *Mutual Gains Bargaining*. I was severely skeptical. I hate gimmicks. I loathe outfits that make you pay a fortune for 3 days of learning what could have been taught in 15 minutes. I wondered if it was really feasible to bring all

parties together and come out with anything even remotely resembling mutual gains. I reluctantly voted for it.

The process proved enormously beneficial. More than
anything, we all had the chance to hear one another. We
listened with respect. We asked questions rather than gave
speeches. We had to look at one another. We recognized
that around the room sat our friends and neighbors. We
gained insights into the feelings that were brought to the
table. We spoke to one another calmly, clearly, and with
conviction.

The process sought to break down barriers. To free us
from seeing ourselves as representing sides. We worked
hard to find common ground. To establish mutually beneficial goals. To establish consensus. Many voices became
one. Many viewpoints were focused as a single vision.
The process was saturated in compromise.

Everyone had to give ground. We soon realized that
common ground is top soil. The best does rise to the top.
The process brought out the best in us. Our vision found
a voice. It was a voice that carried a tune, a carefully
crafted harmony of diverse sounds.

What shocked me the most was something intangible
that happened: We started to feel like a community, a
family. We bargained as if we were truly all friends. At the

end of the process, we all knew what we could sell to the taxpayers of Sag Harbor. We knew what we would have to fight for and what had to be sacrificed. We were in it together, and our strategy reflected that perspective.

We carved out a contract with which everyone felt they had gained. Everyone had been heard. Everyone had been shown respect. Issues were depersonalized. Affirmations were offered where we knew money could not be. We held to a vision that was fair. It was an open and honest process, a free-flowing exchange. Having done the preliminary work of creating a sense of mutuality, we were able to do the painful work of hammering out the details of a contract.

Mutuality means together, shared, we before me. It is not easy to get Americans to think as a we; however, it is crucial to developing communication. One of America's greatest needs is to learn how to think and function as a community, especially as a global community. Self-centeredness destroys communication and erodes love. Me-ism is the downfall of many marriages, friendships, families, and even businesses, congregations, and communities.

We Thinking

Compromise can be overused. Relationships that require constant compromise are fated to falter. We can't always be bargaining. We can't negotiate every little issue. That is what we do when we are getting a divorce. Compromise is essential but should be used sparingly.

Compromise is most effective when it leads to "we thinking," or when two or more people begin to think as a unit. Their outlook immediately takes their partners into consideration. They are confident they can speak for the others. They know and feel known. There is a deep, mutual respect. When we think as a we, we can complete one another's sentences.

We thinking moves beyond compromise. Compromise has been transformed into togetherness, true family, true community. We thinking can only occur in a secure setting, a place where anything can be said and in front of anyone, a context of deep and time-tested love. When we start to think as a we, we can then act as a we. The strength of numbers is well documented. There is nothing stronger than a gathering of good folks who see themselves as a we.

All relationships have conflicts. I remember Christine and my first Christmas. I wanted Christmas to be exactly as my family had practiced. Christine wanted every custom her family had celebrated. In order to accomplish it all, we faced the dilemma of finding another house and 12 more days in December. We worked for days on coming up with a compromise. We were hopelessly deadlocked.

At last, we agreed, we would create a whole new Christmas tradition that was our own. We would have the first ever Bill and Christine Grimbol Christmas, with new customs, new traditions, and new rituals. It would be a fresh start. For the first time in our married life, we were forced to think as a we. It was a joyous and maturing experience. Our first Christmas together was not the disaster we had expected, but a beautiful celebration of a new family.

The Questions

Am I open to compromise? What am I unwilling to compromise? Am I willing to give in or up? Can I think as a we? When? Where? How?

The Prayer

O God, keep me open to compromise. Let me be willing to negotiate. Let me come to any bargaining table with an open heart and mind. Let me be willing to make sacrifices. Let me stand firm when I believe it is necessary. Grant me the courage of faith to think and act as a we. Let me always remember that we are your children—your people. Amen.

A Heart-to-Heart Talk

The genius of communication is the ability
to be both totally honest and totally kind at the
same time.

—*John Powell*

When was the last time you had a heart-to-heart talk? Who
was it with? How did it make you feel? Did you notice any
change in yourself? Was your perspective altered?

In preparing to write this chapter, these were the questions I asked myself. It was a fascinating experience to
remember and then answer these questions.

My last heart-to-heart talk was with my son. It was on
Ash Wednesday. We had lunch together and decided to
go for a drive. As we drove, Justin burst into tears. He
wailed for a full five minutes. He caught me off-guard.
I had no idea he was still in so much pain.

When the tears subsided, he looked at me and said,
"I would give anything to have just one more day with
Mom." I knew the feeling. I also avoided that feeling.
What we did next was to share with one another how

we would spend that one more day, were we given the chance. As you might expect, it was full of doing the simplest of things.

Justin's day with his mother would begin with breakfast at the Candy Kitchen in Bridgehampton, followed by the long drive to a favorite comic book store in Huntington. He would share with her all of his thoughts and feelings about his relationship with Dani, his ex-girlfriend—his pain in having the romance end, his concern about staying friends. He would fill her in on his plans for the fall and his hopes for the future. He would tell her all about the kids from her youth group. He would make her go to McDonald's and a movie, both of which she would probably hate but love doing with him.

My day with Christine would be for us to go for a walk on the ocean and have a long conversation over coffee. We would visit some of her favorite folks from her congregation. We would go for a swim and a whirlpool at the Omni. We would have dinner at The Coast Grill. We would have soft-shell crab. We would sit on a bench at the water and watch the sun set. We would reminisce. We would watch *Mary Tyler Moore* reruns and eat popcorn. I would give her a back rub and a foot massage. We would just hold each other and remember.

A heart-to-heart talk is a miracle. The hearts truly speak. Swollen hearts burst with tears of sorrow, happiness, or joy. The heart tells the truth, the Gospel truth. The heart speaks of only that which matters. The heart releases that information which is sacred. The heart communicates at the deepest level. The heart reveals what has been on the mind for months.

Justin and I had a heart-to-heart on Ash Wednesday 2002. His tears ushered in a conversation of enormous depth and feeling. We let our imaginations have their say. We gave full sway to our emotions. We released our secrets. This can only be done in a relationship of enormous trust and love. The contents of such a dialog must be treated with great care.

We both left that conversation a little lighter, brighter, energized, looser, at ease, in better balance, and more alive. We both left certainly feeling loved—past, present, and future—and a good deal more confident. We both knew the grief was not over, but we were sure of our survival.

Spilling Our Guts

We all hold our emotions in. We try to ignore unsettling thoughts or anxiety-producing issues. We seek to repress those memories that are too painful or emotional to bear recalling. The net result is a spiritual nausea. We think if we stay perfectly still, if we don't move, if we don't go near the thoughts or feelings they will all go away. Wrong! There is only one way nausea disappears. We must get it up and out. We must spill our guts.

Spilling our guts is releasing information that is bothering us, haunting us, nagging at our minds, swarming in our souls. It is freeing what we find troubling or difficult. It is exposing the secret—which ironically, is often not all that secret. It is releasing ourselves from the burden of carrying around the garbage of grief or guilt. It is venting our frustration and fears. Ultimately, it is all about letting go and letting God.

Many folks expend enormous energy trying to hold things in or back. They live like volcanoes. When they finally do erupt, which volcanoes are meant to do, there will be unnecessary destruction. I cannot begin to tell you how much life is lost in trying to restrain our guts, how many days are wasted. The more we try to deny what we truly think, feel, experience, or believe, the sicker and sadder we become.

When good communication provides a safe place and love promises a thorough cleanup, guts can be spilled. We don't have to pretend to be fine when we aren't. We don't have to act as if we are on top of the world when our hearts are stuck in the mire of sorting out life's troubles. We don't have to look like we have all the answers when we are infested by life's big questions.

A Leap of Faith

A heart-to-heart talk is still a risk. It will feel that way. There will be some anxiety, a bit of tension, a mosquito of worry, a prowling fear. Having a heart-to-heart requires a leap of faith and a belief that this person can be trusted to catch us, to hold us up if we fall, and to help with the cleanup.

One cannot underestimate the importance of trust in communication. Trust is what gives communication the freedom of movement. It is like having a good massage, only this time on the heart. The heart feels relaxed and rested, free of tautness and tension, flexible, agile, capable of flight. When the heart can soar, so does the quality of our communication and loving. Both take wing on trust.

It is surprising how often the words *trust* and *faith* can be used interchangeably. Trusting someone is having faith in them. Trusting someone is believing that they are not only reliable but also worthy of respect. Trusting someone is holding the conviction that she has a good soul and means you no harm.

Hold Up

When we entrust our hearts to someone's care, we are asking her to hold something precious. We are not asking for an opinion or judgment. We are not soliciting advice. We are not asking to chat. We are asking for someone to listen and love us. We are asking to be cared about.

We are declaring our need to be held. We want our thoughts to be held in confidence, our feelings in tenderness, our pain in mercy, our needs in respect, our wants and wishes in love. We are asking to be held up for a time, to let us lean, to be offered support, to be allowed to heal.

Being held is healing. It is to be deeply touched. An embrace expresses care and concern and compassion. It is an effort to squeeze away the fear or pain. It offers a rod to help straighten another's spiritual spine.

Remember, when someone says to pull yourself up by your bootstraps, if you try to do just that, you will fall flat on your face. The only way someone can be pulled up by the bootstraps is if she has one person on each side.

There are times when we must ask for support. We need to be held up by the love of others.

A heart-to-heart talk is always an epiphany. The thoughts, feelings, ideas, memories, beliefs, or experiences shared are seen in the brightest of lights. There is great insight and illumination. Voices and visions are clear. Truth becomes transparent. A heart-to-heart talk transports us to eternity, to God's Kingdom, to a safe, secure, and sacred place, to a spot where we stand naked yet feel fully clothed in beauty.

The Questions

Am I in touch with my heart? Who do I allow to touch my heart? What are the risks if I have a heart-to-heart talk? With whom do I long to share such a deep conversation? Why? How can I make it happen?

The Prayer

O God, get me in touch with my heart. Let me touch the hearts of others. Let me serve as your heart to the world. Let my heart beat with your generosity and grace. Let me risk having many heart-to-heart talks with you and with those special folks you have placed in my life. Amen.

Soul Mates

*Friendship is a single soul dwelling in
two bodies.*

—*Aristotle*

It is late August. It has been in the 90s since late July.
The air is limp and sticky. Grass is the color of wheat.
Lousy golfers hit 300-yard drives as the ball kicks up dust
and rolls and rolls and rolls. People are getting irritable.
The hum of air conditioners is universal background
noise. Water usage is restricted. Every day there is a
threatened power outage.

Black bear clouds form in the Western sky. The wind
picks up. The first drops of rain are huge, like bubbles.
The earth goes polka dot. Thunder rumbles, and light-
ning flashes. A downpour falls, a steady rain for two full
hours with at least two inches accumulation, and a blissful drop in temperature. The air is fresh and clean and
70 degrees. The sky turns from bleached blue to neon.
The sun sparkles rather than slumps. Everyone is out for
a walk or bike ride or just to breathe the air.

This is what it feels like to find a soul mate—fresh, clean, as if we have come home, been born again, entered heaven. All is calm. All is bright. We can breathe easily. We feel relaxed and renewed. We are centered. We are grounded in grace.

When I was young, I did not believe there was such a thing as a soul mate. At 52, I think there are all kinds of soul mates. A mate can be a soul mate. A sibling can be. All true friends are soul mates. A neighbor, stranger, teacher, author, composer, choreographer—anyone who speaks to your soul can be a soul mate. Soul mates are those folks in our lives who connect with us on an eternal basis. They reveal the heaven inside and outside us.

Some soul mates we have known for a lifetime, some for only a moment. Traditionally, we think of soul mates as life partners, people with whom we will share the journey. I like to think of a soul mate as anyone who makes an indelible imprint on our heart, mind, and soul; someone who is literally unforgettable; someone who carves his or her initials in our spiritual skin.

Soul mates lift the veil. They puncture the phoniness. They expose the truth, the Gospel truth. They reveal the essence. They lift up the best. They inspire and invite maturation. They ignite faith. Soul mates make our lives better, smarter, wiser, and fuller. In their presence, we become more noticeably God's. We function as God's beloved. We act as if we have received God's grace—because we have.

Believing Is Seeing

Soul mates believe in us. They communicate this faith in us. They let us know we are worthy of their trust and respect. They value our ideas. They consider our opinion important. They accept our criticism. They welcome our advice. Soul mates tell us, in no uncertain terms, that we are held in high regard, that we are esteemed, that we are honored.

As a result of their belief in us, soul mates can see inside us. They know our heart's desire. They can read our minds. They are in touch with our feelings. They have wandered the caverns of our soul. A soul mate knows us, understands us, feels empathy and compassion for us, and encourages and inspires us. A soul mate can see who we are as well as who we can become. A soul mate will bring out the very best of who we are.

Just One Look

I remember waiting for the airport bus to arrive at the St. Olaf College Campus Center. The bus would come at noon. I had been stationed on the Center steps, suitcase at my side, since 8 A.M. It was my first fall break, my first visit home as a college man, and I was not about to miss that damn bus. So there I sat, trying to look casual for four full hours.

A senior I knew of but had never met approached. I don't recall his name, but his face is etched on my memory: his bright blue eyes, his white blond Scandinavian hair, his ruddy cheeks, his smile, his perfect white Edina teeth. He looked at me knowingly and said "Have a great fall break. It is always good to get home. The bus will be here at noon. You can count on it."

I wanted to run and kiss him but just nodded instead. I was so appreciative of his gesture. For that one moment, we were soul mates. He knew me as well as anyone on the planet at that moment. He sought to be my friend, and on that day, he was my best friend. He was exactly who I needed, saying exactly what I longed to hear said.

The tension departed, as did the embarrassment. I calmly waited for the bus, which came right on time. I had a great fall break. I saw him a few more times that year, and we always nodded at one another. We never spoke again, just exchanged looks, a recognition of being human beings who are, indeed, in this together.

The Face of God

I believe that God has a hand in choosing some of our soul mates but not all of them and not when or where they will appear. I have never liked the notion of God as marionette master and we the string-laced puppets. I think God chooses when to show himself/herself, when to reveal his/her wants or wishes, when to inspire or call or challenge, when to expose his/her nature, and when to offer us a slice of grace.

Several years ago I needed to go to Sloan-Kettering for an evaluation of a large nodule on my vocal cord. There was a chance it might be cancerous. A member of my congregation arranged for me to see a top specialist in throat cancers.

The bus to New York City was jammed to capacity. It was windy and wet outside, and the traffic was a snarling mess. I tried to use the bathroom on the bus and almost got a concussion. I tried to read, but I was too anxious. My voice was my livelihood. Public speaking had always been what I considered my greatest talent. I was, in a word, terrified.

I arrived safely at the hospital, filled out the necessary paperwork, and went to find my doctor's office on the third floor. Because I was a full hour early, I decided to wander the halls for a bit. I had heard so much about Sloan-Kettering, and I wanted to check it out.

It was huge. For all of its obvious efforts to be welcoming, it remained cold. Everywhere I looked, I saw lines of people. Though Sloan-Kettering is well known as a cancer hospital, it is still striking to see so many young bald heads, hollow cheeks, and parchment-thin skin. As I turned a corner, I was shocked to see a row of wheelchairs with kids—children as young as two and some into their teens—awaiting tests and treatments.

Someone had just farted. The kids were all laughing hysterically and pointing fingers at one another. I can recall their faces as easily as that of my own son's. There they were, the laughing faces of God. These tough, courageous little kids were having a belly laugh over a fart.

I was swept by peace. My faith went from flimsy to full, from limp to firm. My panic left. I was nervous, but no more so than these young ones. I saw in their faces a genuine appreciation for life, for something as simple as a laugh and something as silly as a fart. These youngsters were my momentary soul mates, reminding me of God's presence, telling me of God's love, speaking God's favorite words: "Do not be afraid!"

I think of soul mates as earth angels. These are the folks who make us feel like we are in heaven. Better yet, they make us believe we deserve to be there.

The Questions
Who are my soul mates? When have I seen the face of God? Can I choose to be a soul mate? Who would I choose to be my soul mate?

The Prayer
O God, I give you great thanks for my soul mates, the friends who have shown they know me inside out and hold my heart carefully in cupped hands, the strangers who have shown me a look of love or imparted words of great wisdom, those sweet souls who have crawled deep inside me and carved an eternal niche in my heart. Amen.

Just Be Yourself

Be yourself. No one can ever tell you you're doing it wrong.

—James Leo Herlihy

When my son, Justin, was around age two, he fell in love with birthday parties. He had his on April 7, and four of his little friends were to have theirs during May and June. Each invitation brought wide smiles and whoops of glee. He dutifully went with his mother to buy each child a gift. He would leave the house for each party looking happy and spiffy. He would return from each party crestfallen.

The problem seemed to be that Justin believed each of these parties was for him. A birthday meant *his* birthday. The fact that four other kids had caught on to the idea had pleased him to no end. He would even sing, "Happy birthday to me!" at the top of his lungs at each party. He was also quite confident that the present he had carefully chosen would be willingly returned to him on this the second, third, fourth, and fifth celebration of his birthday.

Justin was devastated by the bad news. Other kids had birthdays, too. It wasn't until he was five that he came to enjoy attending someone else's birthday party.

In Christian Scripture, Christ encourages his followers to become like children. Becoming like children means many different things to many different people. It is one of those admonitions Jesus failed to spell out in detail. He left a lot of room for interpretation.

For me, one of the key features of childlikeness is to genuinely like who you are. Children tend to enjoy themselves. They are proud of their talents. Most kids readily claim to be gifted. If you ask a bunch of elementary-age youngsters to tell you what they are good at, most of the time they are quick with an avalanche of answers.

I must admit that there are those children who tragically have their affinity for self knocked out of them at an early age. Emotional and physical abuse and neglect can demolish that raw, early confidence and refreshing conceit. Only if a child is shown hate or disgust, will a child relinquish his or her liking of self.

It is adolescence that turns this innate liking into acute skepticism. It is adolescence where the endless worrying about how I look, sound, and act arises and where all questions of self-worth and value are placed in the hands of ruthlessly competitive peers. During the emotional and relational combat of adolescence, the spontaneous liking of self tends to dwindle—so much so that there is often nothing left but an image, and that image may bear no resemblance to the lovely child that once flourished inside.

Childlikeness is centered in liking yourself, in seeing no reason for *not* celebrating one's birthday a minimum of five times. Childlikeness is not naïveté or ignorance. It is a basic belief that "I am likeable and loveable." Most children who have received even a modicum of good parenting approach life as a divine right. They see themselves as worthy recipients of God's many gifts.

Children celebrate who they are. They are honest, genuine, and natural. They tell it like it is. They can be silly or sad at a moment's notice. Teardrops can be replaced by wild raucous laughter in a second.

Children go with the flow. They live each day as if it were the first. They have no conception of last. They are free, free to be who God created them to be; free to think, feel, and believe that the sky can be pink and the grass bright orange; free to be creative.

Celebrating Our Imperfections

I am not handy. I own one tool, a hammer. It is a dainty hammer. I use it to hang pictures, which is the extent of my handiness. I have been told I should take a handyman course. I have thought about it—for about four minutes. I decided it would not be fair to take a course from a teacher who would either have a nervous breakdown or be charged with murder trying to teach me.

For a long time, I was embarrassed by the fact that I could not do much with my hands. When asked to fix something, I would grow quiet, frustrated, and enraged. I wasn't a man's man. I felt guilty and inadequate. I will admit to making a few efforts at repair. The cost of repairing my repairs was nearly double. In one case, the plumber started to laugh uproariously, as did my wife and son. I failed to find the humor in having run the water after removing the elbow pipe below the sink.

About 7 years ago, at the age of 45, I had an epiphany. I decided that I could care less if I was handy. I did lots of things well. I could write, paint, preach, teach, and counsel. So what if I could not build an addition or repair a toilet? I would have to pay for those services or ask friends for help. I soon realized that if I asked for assistance, many were glad to offer it, often in gratitude for other services I had rendered them—and for free.

If we are to celebrate our selves, we must start with our imperfections. We must learn to embrace those parts of our selves we find embarrassing. We need to laugh at our weaknesses and speak easily of our flaws. We must be willing to name our flops and address our mistakes.

We were never meant to be perfect. Perfectionism is a curse. It is demoralizing. It robs us of energy. It eliminates celebration. Perfectionists are never ready to celebrate. They always need more work. They are never enough. In order to celebrate being exactly who and what we are, we must be ready to claim the reality of our imperfections.

Celebrating Our Gifts

Charlie lived in my childhood neighborhood. He was a great gardener. Neighbors would bargain with him for a few ears of corn or a juicy tomato or one of his sweet melons. He also tended a magnificent bed of flowers. His roses were spectacular, as were his spring tulips. Several neighborhood brides carried Charlie's flowers down the aisle.

Charlie's garden became famous—only in our neighborhood, of course, but that was enough for Charlie.

He became so proud of his produce and reputation that each spring he would hold a grand opening, complete with a ribbon-cutting ceremony. The neighbors would all gather and applaud, and Charlie would take a bow. Charlie was 91 years old.

We are all gifted. This is true. It is vital that we know and name our gifts. It is crucial that we do not diminish the importance of a gift simply because our culture fails to take note. Our gift can be as simple as being a good listener or gift shopper. It can range from being a wonderful cook to a terrific parent. It can be notable as being a fine musician or as seemingly insignificant as having a fine sense of humor.

What *is* important is recognizing our gifts, lifting them up for others to see and hear and know, being proud, taking note that we do this well, and asking others to notice. Celebration is not shy. It will not hide a talent under a bushel. Celebrating our gifts means putting those talents and abilities under the spotlight. It means enjoying the applause—even if we are the only one clapping.

When we celebrate our gifts, I suspect it is pleasing to God. We are indirectly affirming God. I propose that God would add a standing ovation to the celebration.

Celebrating Our Givens

What is a given? It is something over which we have little to no control. Our height, our looks, our family, our IQ, our inclinations—these are all givens. There is a good deal in life that we must simply accept. These are God's terms.

There can be no true celebration of who we are unless there is first an acceptance of these God-given terms. We must embrace the boundaries and borders of our birth, as well as the opportunities to actualize our wishes and dreams. Celebration is a careful balance.

Celebration is not a declaration of invincibility or omnipotence. On the contrary, what we celebrate is being human. We celebrate all that it means to be human— the tears of sorrow and joy, the extraordinary accomplishments, the ordinary failures, the courage to meet the challenge, the wisdom to ask for help, the soaring of youth, the settling of adulthood, and the marvelous melting of old age. We embrace and celebrate it all.

If we are to be fully capable of love, we must be ready to celebrate who we are. We must like ourselves. We must know ourselves. We must trust and respect ourselves. We must find ourselves to be worthy of love and respect. We must believe ourselves to be admirable.

When we know we are loveable, we are free to love.
When we freely love, life itself becomes a celebration.

The Questions
*Do I love myself? When? Where? How? Why or why not?
What would it mean for me to celebrate me? When was the
last time I celebrated me? What are my gifts? I consider
myself to be a gifted ...*

The Prayer
*O God, let me celebrate who I am. Let me rejoice in my
limits and my gifts. Let me dance at the possibilities, as
well as for those that have passed. Let me sing praises to
myself, a melody of knowing that I am a miracle created
by a most gracious God. Amen.*

An Expanding Universe

Only love can be divided endlessly
and still not diminish.

—*Anne Morrow Lindbergh*

I have worked with youth for 25 years. I love adolescents.
I love the turbulence. I love the drama. I love the wild-
eyed optimism. I love the raging despair. I will admit that
it is often like living on the set of *As the World Turns*, but
I have come to appreciate how adolescence is a crash-
course in love.

There is one aspect of adolescence with which I am
weary. I don't hate it. I know I have to hear all about it.
I must take it ever so seriously. But, man, has it gotten
boring to hear about the greatest love anyone has ever
known, that first all-consuming passion, the Great Fall of
falling in love. The eyes that gaze at only one other set of
eyes, as if the rest of the world had disappeared, along
with the entire population.

Max and Karla are my latest star-crossed lovers. They
are both 17 and in my youth group. They are hopelessly

infatuated with one another. They see each other before school, during school, and every minute they can after school. When not in face-to-face contact, they are on the phone. Even after a full day of being together, the first thing they do when home is, yes, you guessed it, call one another. The sole issue of each and every day is "Do you love me?" and "How much?"

What is most disturbing about their relationship is their shrinkage as individuals. Both ignore their friends. Both have no time for family. They speak of nothing else but each other. They are interested in nothing else. Karla was once an avid reader, and Max, a devout musician. Books and guitars have fallen to the wayside. When I am in their presence, I feel as though I am not there. Ironically, in many respects, neither are they.

Max and Karla would swear that what they have is true love. They have found the holy grail. They have discovered their soul mate. None of it is true. True love does not result in shrinking the self. True love does not require the world to evaporate. True love does not exclude others.

True love is a celebration. It celebrates a love that expands our universe and creates new hopes and dreams, friends, and even deeper bonds. True love opens our eyes and hearts and minds even wider. True love encourages us to welcome the world. True love is anything but a private universe. True love grants us the courage to go public.

True love offers the recipient an energy boost, a spirit lift. It ignites the desire to make a difference and convinces us we can do it if we try. True love is not just for two. It is for everyone. It makes the world a better place for all.

A Passion for Compassion

Most of what I know about love, I learned from my mother. She was my best teacher. My father also taught a class or two, but he didn't offer as much insight as my mother did.

My mother's life has been a celebration of compassion. She has a passion for compassion, a fervent belief that we must care deeply about the needs of others. Admittedly, at times she did go overboard, but in today's callous and selfish world, I have a deep appreciation for her focus on others.

I recall the many summer nights when the porch ladies would gather on our front porch. Mom and her neighborhood friends swapped lives over lemonade and popcorn and the blissfully cool breezes off Lake Michigan, chattering merrily over the day's or week's events, sharing the frustrations and successes of marriage and family, venting worries and fears, offering one another advice and assurances, and always laughing.

When Grandpa died suddenly of a heart attack, the porch ladies took over my mother's life. They cooked, cleaned, did the wash, and entertained my sister and me. They made sure Mom had every moment she needed to heal. They also gathered on that same porch and cried with her—many nights and many tears.

Love enables compassion. Love encourages it. Love enhances it. When we know love, when we have basked in its warmth and been showered with its gifts, and when we have savored its joys, we want to share it. We especially want to offer it to someone who needs it, someone in pain, someone lost or lonely, someone sinking in sadness.

Loving people are compassionate people. They are good listeners. They care. They offer excellent counsel. They feel with us. They have good insight. They are sensitive and intuitive. They climb inside our heart and mind. They inhabit our soul. They willingly walk a mile in our shoes. They are like my mom—or any one of the porch ladies.

A Catalyst to Care

Adolescents have a good eye. They know immediately if an adult really cares or is just doing his job or playing a role. They have excellent radar for the phony. They know when they are being patronized. They know when the love shown is too sweet, too much, or too temporary. They know when words ring hollow, when lips say one thing but detached, distant eyes say something else.

Adolescents demand caring from adults. Without it, they will not perform. They won't be honest. They will not be candid. They will not put forth much effort. They won't show excitement. They will refuse to participate or do so begrudgingly. They will not show their stuff. They themselves will not be real. They won't let you see their funny side or their wild side or their sad and vulnerable side. They will only give you their "I'm okay" side.

For an adolescent, caring is the acid test of love. Only if you care about me, will I even consider that you might love me. If I fail to see you care, if I do not experience your genuine interest and kindness, then I will not open up to you. I may let you in, but not inside, not where it counts. You may have gotten through the door, but I will keep you in the hallway.

Love is a celebration of caring. It is caring about everything in someone's life, his needs, his dreams, his anxiety and fear, his displays of courage, his noble efforts, and his staggering defeats. Love creeps into every nook and cranny. Love cares about the big picture as well as the tiniest detail.

Really Concerned

One of the great gifts of being an adult is that we have gotten pretty good at knowing who our real friends are. We know which folks we can count on in a crisis, for help with the boring chore, or for support over the long haul. We know which friends will be there, who will respond to the late-night call, who will listen to a mess of a story, who will take our silly problem seriously. We even know who will give us the gift of their absence.

Our true friends express their concern. They do so in a million ways. They simply let us know we matter. They get upset to see us upset. If they see us making stupid choices, they worry. If they witness us compromising our health or cherished relationships, they will take the risk of speaking up. They offer criticism with kindness and warnings without threats. And they never stop telling us that we are loved.

True friends show their love. We don't need to guess about it. We see it. We hear it. We feel it. It shows in their eyes. Their eyes speak of their love for us. They are focused and attentive. They take note of every little nuance or action. They observe us with compassion and care and genuine concern. Only from a true friend can I hear the words, "I am really concerned!" and know that I must stop and listen. I must take this concern seriously. This concern is an expression of real love, the genuine article.

The Questions
Is my love growing? Am I more mature in my loving? Has my compassion deepened? Am I kinder, more caring? Am I truly concerned for others?

The Prayer
O God, let me grow. Let me mature. Let my spirit soar. Widen my universe. Deepen my compassion. Expand my loving and forgiving. Let me reach out for my neighbor as well as for the stars. Let me be more—more like you, more of you, more gracious, more full of grace. Amen.

Homecoming

Home is a place you grow up wanting to leave,
and grow old wanting to get back to.

—*John Ed Pearce (in the* Louisville Courier-
Journal Magazine*)*

The letter arrived yesterday—the announcement of my
twenty-fifth high school reunion. I stared at the words in
disbelief. I had graduated in 1967 from William Horlick
High School in Racine, Wisconsin. It was now 1992. I
could not believe the swiftness of time's passing. Twenty-
five years had passed in what felt like 25 minutes—the
length of a sitcom.

I really wanted to go … but …. I had put on weight—
a lot of weight. My 32-inch waist was now 42. I had male
pattern baldness. My skin had recently developed rosacea.
The one thing I had managed to keep of my youth was
acne. I was a minister in a small church on a tiny island.
I had published one little book called *Why Should I
Care?*—a fitting title for my feelings about attending this
reunion. Still, the fact was, I did care. A lot. Too much.

I traveled back to Racine for the event. I got my hair cut and some new clothes. I had tried to lose some weight, but managed to add five pounds. Up until a few minutes before the event was to begin, I was not sure I would attend. Geez, I wasn't even this vain in high school. I was amazed at how insecure I felt about not being at my best—at least physically. I felt 16 again.

When I walked into the Racine Country Club, I immediately spotted Jerry Filicetti. We had not seen one another in 25 years. We smiled and hugged and dove into catching up. Then I saw Spinksy. He had a gut to match my own. Luke and Boz and Heinkel, Marita and Mary and Sharon—friends with whom I had shared my growing up, my family were also there. I was awed by the level of love I felt, the ease, the comfort of being in their company. These people were my home.

We had all changed physically, emotionally, and spiritually. Some of us had been spectacularly successful, some less so, some not at all. Nobody cared. Nobody cared about the appearances. Nobody was competing any more. In the eye of memory, we all looked great.

I had been foolish to worry about my image. I had been stupid to think I had to make an impression—or that I could. These people were not easily impressed.

They knew the real me, inside and out. They loved me in spite of myself. They loved what we were together—the sweetness of those times, the goodness of those days, and the absence of fear. Terror was unheard of. The blissful cockiness of youth reigned.

At my twenty-fifth high school reunion, I came home. Home to the realization of my aging. Home to my imperfections. Home to being much more than an impression, an image, a success, an author. Home to being just me, a me who was enough—more than enough—a me remembered with love, a me who belonged, a me rooted in Racine.

I came home to my hometown and to the people who made me feel at home. But most of all, I came home to my self. I came home to Billy Grimbol, son of Hedy and Lenny Grimbol, brother to Jackie. Not so bad. Not bad at all. And God saw him, and God said "He is very good."

Homesick

All sickness is homesickness. *Dis-ease* means to be out of ease with life. We are most ill at ease when trying to prove ourselves, when trying to be a somebody, when trying to make a name. We lose our balance in our crazed efforts to be winners. Our insane fear of being a loser drives us into hiding. We become the me nobody knows. We play a role for so long, a part, that we begin to believe in our image and buy into our own hype. We forget who we are. We sell our soul.

Losing *home* is a tragedy. It is also predictable. It seems to be our spiritual destiny. Somehow we must get lost before we can be found. We must walk away from all we know. We must turn our backs on what defines our essence and head out in search of another self, someone more powerful, more charismatic, a somebody without the flaws, somebody who will sail through life with the greatest of ease.

We never find this somebody else. Or if we do, we don't like him or her much. This other person is incapable of love and has no faith and few hopes. This other person makes us feel sick to our stomachs and nauseated by his phoniness and pretensions. This other self is a jerk, demanding and needy and with an insatiable appetite for attention. We are worn out by this other person. We are sick and tired of being him or her.

We yearn for home. The longing for home is also part of our spiritual nature. We can't wait to be back in familiar surroundings, where it is okay to be ordinary, vulnerable, a flop, a slob, a pest, a royal pain, sweet and kind, tender and loving, known to jump for joy and leap for faith. We want to be back in a context where we are free to be ourselves, our true selves, human beings in the raw.

Homework

Many of us have gotten ourselves hopelessly lost—stranded on a distant planet, far removed from our true selves, out of touch with our hearts and with our God.

We are in trouble, anxious, chronically empty and exhausted, worried sick. We are listless, lack energy or excitement, and know something is terribly wrong but are not able to put a finger on it.

We feel numb. Catatonic. When someone asks us how we are, we tell them what we are doing. We don't know how we are. We haven't a clue what we are feeling. Our thoughts are like bug wings, thin and brittle and easily ripped to shreds. Our faith is no more than a trickle, a few drops of dogma or doctrine, nothing that flows, nothing that could sustain life.

Coming home spiritually takes work, homework, time to get to know ourselves again. It requires getting reacquainted with our souls and our God, renewing our prayer life, and silence, stillness, and solitude. It requires finding opportunities for worship and service, putting someone else's needs ahead of our own, making a sacrifice, and picking up our crosses and carrying them. It requires following the leader—God.

Coming home, home to ourselves, home to our God, home to our calling, home to our life, home to life—this is the work of the human spirit in consort with the Divine Spirit. This is spiritual homework. This is the work of surrender—letting go of the foolish effort to be somebody else, letting ourselves get to know the self God created.

The Questions
Am I at home with myself? With God? When do I feel most alienated? Why? How do I lose myself? How do I choose to become an alien? What is my homework for today?

The Prayer
O God, lead me back home to you. Let me warm myself at your hearth. Let me feed my soul with your food. Let me rest in your arms. Let me feel safe. Let me know true security. Prepare me for the journey. Lead me back to love. Amen.

Follow That Star!

A rock pile ceases to be a rock pile the moment a single man contemplates it, bearing within him the image of a cathedral.

—*Antoine De Saint-Exupery (*Flight to Arras*)*

We are God's beloved children. Consider that. For just a few minutes, take that information in. Absorb it. Float around in it. We are loved beyond measure. We are encased in forgiveness. We are held tightly by grace.

God's children know how to celebrate. They exult in every dawn. They give thanks at every dusk. They cherish their days. They seek to fill them with love. They seek to be true to their callings. They live their longings and questions. They are inspired by hope. Their hope creates dreams. God's children have faith they will actualize their dreams.

God's children do not wish for trivial or foolish things. Their hope is in service to God. Their dreams are of making miracles happen, building the Kingdom, creating enduring intimate relationships, deepening their contact with God.

God's children celebrate dreams that make the world a saner and safer place to live, dreams that bring peace, dreams that build bridges and open doors, dreams that unite folks, dreams that keep us alive with hope, full of faith, living to love, loving to live.

God's children dream dreams that require risk—the risk of rejecting the world, the risk of following God. God's children dream dreams that move us, that make us mature, that change our perspective, and that enable us to grow. Dreams force us to leave the familiar, to reach, to go out, to expand our selves and our world, to open our arms wide enough to receive God. Dreams keep all things new, keep life fresh, ripe, ready to receive, primed for service, courageous enough to sacrifice, and wise enough to surrender.

When we accept our status, we are God's *beloved.* We dream big. We live small. Our love and our loving yearn to stretch and grow. We adore change. We are willing to compromise. We take joy from the journey. We revel in the magnificence of God's Creation. We rejoice in learning. We dive into the midst of mystery. We believe in miracles.

Risky Business

My mother and father both loved me equally. I have always known that. My father, however, always wanted me to play it safe—nothing wild, nothing risky. Middle-of-the-road was the safest bet. Keep people happy. Play your cards conservatively.

Mom, on the other hand, gave me another message. It did not come in words—I don't think she liked the idea of disagreeing with Dad. But it was in her eyes—the twinkling delight she took when I announced some crazy plan or scheme or idea. Mom loved it when I took chances. She got a kick out of my willingness to go for broke.

Mom's was the deeper love. It was not greater, just more spiritual. It came from her heart, not her head. Maybe I was doing or being what she had always dreamed. Maybe I made her proud. I think it was that she wanted me to try, to make the attempt, to know I was good enough. Mom gave me my first taste of grace. It was sweet.

Love celebrates our dreams, ignites them, inspires them. Love gives us the kick or push, makes us try, grants us the faith that we can do it, that we can be it. Love enables our dreams to come true. We take risks, knowing that if we fall, we will bounce. Love forms the cushion. Love removes the fear of the fall.

The Wisdom Business

The Three Kings of Christmas fame, the Magi, were not actually kings. They were not magicians. Most likely, they were astrologers. They watched the heavens. They noted the movements of planets and the configurations of stars. They looked for signs, for messages from God, for something that would make them gasp, take their breath away, leave them reborn.

A bright star lit the skies. It was huge. Many believe it was a real event, a once-in-a-lifetime spectacle of starlight, the result of planet placement. Whatever the case, many saw it, but few took it to mean much. These three foreigners chose to follow. They left what they were doing, packed up their bags, and moved on.

Why? What made them follow? Who knows! Maybe it was the emptiness of their lives where they lived. Maybe it was the lack of meaning or the void of intimacy in their lives. Maybe it was like being a storm-chaser and this star was the big one. They could not resist. Maybe it was a matter of faith, a deep belief that this was a sign from God. Maybe it was the conviction that the stars had something to say and God was doing the telling.

Three astrologers set off to follow a star. We call them wise, but the world of their time must have thought them to be idiots. They set off on a journey of faith. They wanted to see for themselves where this would lead. They wanted to see what would be at the end of this rainbow. They wanted to know what story this mammoth star had to tell.

Be it taken as a history or myth, this is a marvelous story. It is a tale of transformation. Three men embark on a perilous trip. They have everything to lose and maybe nothing to gain. The world mocks them.

What do they find? A stable with a mother and a father and a babe in a lowly manger, surrounded by stinking animals and a cast of characters that looked like a traveling circus. Three foreigners knelt, offered gifts, and sang praises. Three men saw this little family in a whole different light—star light. It made all the difference. It changed the world.

Dreams are risks. Dreams move us. Dreams initiate change. Dreams cultivate growth. Dreams yield transformation. Dreams do not make us better. They make us wiser.

If we know we are loved and if we love ourselves and our neighbors, our lives and our world, and our God, we will have no choice but to dream many dreams. We will dream often. We will dream because it expresses this love. It speaks of our passion. It declares our lust for life.

The Questions
What dreams have turned into nightmares? What dreams have I fulfilled? What dreams do I hope to fulfill?

The Prayer
O God, let me dream. Big and tiny dreams. Dreams of doing and being. Dreams that will set my heart on fire. That ignite my soul with passion. That fill my days with zest. That keep me fresh. That keep me wishing and hoping and longing for the stretch, the expansion of my being, the widening of my mercy, and the loosening of my love. Let me flex my muscle, which is my faith in you. Amen.

Creating a Life

When love and skill work together,
expect a masterpiece.

—John Ruskin

This is a summation of a conversation I had with a young man in my congregation who came to me complaining of depression. It was the summer following his senior year in college. He had graduated with honors, having made the Dean's List all four years. He was in love with a beautiful girl. He was sorting through several corporate job offers. His family was loving and supportive. He had a throng of friends. I will call him Brad.

"I don't think you are depressed, Brad."

"Then what am I?"

"I'm not sure. I have some ideas I might throw your way."

"Go ahead. Toss."

"I think you may be bored. I get the sense that you have everything everyone else wants you to have and expects you to have. But you feel like there is something missing. Whatever that something is, without it, you feel lonely and lost. I get the feeling you are very sad."

"Isn't that depression?"

"It can be. But in your case, I don't think so. I think it is more spiritual."

"Spiritual?!"

"Don't get shook. By *spiritual,* I mean your perspective on life. How you see yourself and your world. What gives your life meaning and hope? What is your purpose? Your calling?"

"Calling? Like to the ministry?"

"No, calling as in what you believe God means for you to be doing … and being."

"I just spent four years becoming a master of the computer."

"I know, but I suspect it holds little interest for you. I would guess that you would rather be pursuing piano, learning to compose, and creating music."

"That is just a hobby."

"Is it?"

"Well, I can't just turn my back on my education."

"Can you turn your back on your music?"

At this point Brad began to weep. We spent a good 15 minutes in silence. When the conversation resumed, this is what Brad had to say:

"I have never loved myself enough to make my own choices. I have always wanted to keep everyone happy. I wanted to be a success, a big success. Computers seemed like just the ticket. Now you are telling me that without my music, I will have a lifetime of boredom. What a choice! How can I make such a choice? Any way I go, I will be upsetting someone."

"Brad, let me ask you a tough question. I don't mean it to sound all religious, but what would disappoint God?"

"No question. If I did not give music a try. If I just squandered this gift. Pastor Bill, I have always wanted to write the score for a Broadway musical. Crazy, huh?"

"No. Crazy not to try. Your life is yours to create. You're at a vital juncture here. Choices have to be made. Tough decisions. Ultimately, you will be deciding if you are going to live your life or someone else's."

That summer, Brad made the decision to continue his education—in music. He would spend a year working to earn the money to start at Carnegie-Mellon, a school with an excellent reputation in musical theater. He would, in a literal sense, be starting all over, only this time he was aware that he needed to keep himself happy, and, in so doing, he was confident about pleasing God.

His decision would not please everyone. A good decision never does. It was Brad's choice. It was his life. The sole issue was if it were right for him. He believed it was. For those who questioned him, he only asked for their support. Most folks, even if they believe a decision to be poorly made, will rise to the occasion when asked for support. Brad ultimately got what he needed. He made his own decision. He got the support of family and friends—even if some of that support was lukewarm.

We create our lives. We create them by making choices. We create them by making decisions. We are a product of our attitude and perspective, a reflection of our expectations and those we care about. If we fail to love ourselves, our true selves, we cannot possibly feel good with the life we choose. We may not be destined for failure, but we are certainly not headed in the direction of happiness.

Love Makes Good Choices

Life is jammed with choices. It is not easy to make good choices. It takes time to think, to listen carefully to our heart, to be true to our soul.

Making good choices is made even harder by the world we live in. The world likes quick choices. Easy choices. Black-and-white choices. Pain-free choices. Choices that show a profit. Choices that have something in it for me-me-me.

Here are some helpful questions to ask in determining what makes for a good choice:

- Am I being honest with myself?
- Is it thoughtful of others but not made by them?
- Does it takes all the time it needs to be made?
- Does it consider the consequences—physical, emotional, relational, as well as spiritual?
- Will it enable me to mature?
- Does it have the possibility of making me happy?
- Is it in service to my understanding of God?
- Will it help to build the Kingdom?

- Can I be genuinely proud of making it?
- Will I be able to handle any criticism I might receive?
- Does it expresses my faith, values, and ethics?
- Have I prayed over it?

Making good choices is a skill. It is a skill we can only learn if we know we are loved by God, if we accept God's Grace, and if we know we must first love ourselves.

Love Makes Good Things Happen

When we love ourselves, when we are loved and love our friends and family, when we have faith in the love of God, and when we love life, good things are bound to happen.

No, we will not have a problem-free or pain-free existence. We will know our fair share of sorrow and loss. We may get hit by unexpected or undeserved tragedy. But we will know good things because we are looking for them, seeking them, and creating them. We are making them happen by making good choices, by living a good life, and by having faith in life's goodness.

Love creates energy. Love creates attitude. Love creates a will, a motivation, a discipline. Love creates the spirit, the faith, the hope. Love creates a genuine good life, a life of feeling good, of being good, and of doing good. Love creates a life that expects and get miracles of all kinds.

Love Makes Love with Life

What Brad was missing was passion. He was bored, bored to death. What had died was his music. His music was his passion. Computers were a means of making money, not a means of enjoying life. Only music could provide him with joy. If Brad was to know joy in his life, he would need to find room, a living room, for music in his life.

Love is passion. We need to be passionate about our gifts, our talents, and our callings. We need to be passionate about our relationships, whether romantic or friendship, family or stranger. We need to live our lives with passion. Love is an art. Life is an art. We express our souls with the lives we create.

Think of it this way: We create a life. Just as it takes passion to make a baby, it takes spiritual passion to make a life. It takes a full investment of who and what we are, an open and receptive soul, and a committed heart and mind. It takes patience, perseverance, and practice—tons of practice by daily decisions—an endless cycle of life-transforming choices.

Creating a life should be a joy. It is a mystery being unraveled, a miracle in the making, a sacred yarn being spun. Our lives were never meant to be endured or reduced to just making a living. Life is a passion, an art, a painting, a play, a song. It is God speaking through us.

Each of us is a revelation, an epiphany, an expression of God's Grace. Each of us is worthy of God's gallery. Each of us bears God's signature. We are a masterpiece. A classic. A work of genius.

Imagine the difference in our living if we were to live with such passion, believing we were co-Creators called and commissioned by God. Just imagine.

The Questions

Am I good at making decisions? Have I made some poor decisions? What have I learned from making a bad decision? Or, a good one? What kind of life am I creating for myself? What would I like to create? How might God use me? How can I further the Creation?

The Prayer

O God, let me create. Let me create a life that is worthy of you. Let me create a life that is full—full of love and laughter, of honest tears and genuine grief, of forgiveness and more forgiveness. Let me create a passionate living true to my callings, from the heart, dedicated to following your will, and jammed with the wisdom of surrendering. O God, you have given me dominion over all the earth. Let my dominion reflect my gracious gratitude. Let it explode with love. Let it drape this good earth with a good life of doing and being good. Amen.

Committed to an Institution

One advantage of marriage is that, when you fall out of love with him or he falls out of love with you, it keeps you together until you fall in again.

—Judith Viorst

I found marriage to be hard work—rewarding but tough. We had sweet periods of satisfaction. We triumphed over adversity. We created hopes and dreams. We fought. We forgave. We fought. We held grudges. I pouted. Christine raged. We went through spells of boredom. We got sick of one another. We found each other irritating. We fell in love again.

What makes marriage hard is that it takes place in life. Life itself can be difficult. Marriage also takes place between two people, two lives, two sets of families, histories, traditions, rituals, and perspectives. Marriage is always a work in progress. The work is in merging, in finding common ground, in creating a vision that reflects four eyes.

I had a volatile marriage. Christine and I were passionate people—stubborn, intense, and sensitive. We both had tempers and strong opinions. We were also nothing alike. I will give you an example: vacations. I like country inns with no phones or television; long, leisurely drives down country lanes; and eating in cute, cozy, family-style restaurants. Christine liked good hotels with pools, saunas, and cable; eating in good restaurants with gourmet cuisine; and driving fast and freeways.

I will admit we came to the point of splitting more than once. On one occasion, we went so far as to divvy up the furniture. What kept us together? Our vows. Our belief in the institution of marriage. Our son. Our families. Not wanting to damage anyone. Our long historical commitment to each other (we had been together as a couple for 25 years). Our faith. Down deep we both believed the love would keep re-igniting.

We live in a culture that has grown lazy with commitments. We walk away from our vows with casual ease. We have grown numb to divorce. Breakups are almost expected and certainly predicted. We are a culture that accepts lies as standard practice. We don't say what we mean. We don't mean what we say. We say what is convenient, what gets us off the hook, or what costs the least. Vows are thought of as old-fashioned.

My grandmother told me that the good old days were better because the people were better. She may have been right. We need to take a long, hard look at what it means to keep a vow and what it means to us to make a commitment, whether in work, friendship and family, community and congregation, or our world. Do we keep our promises? Do we fulfill our commitments? Are we true to our word?

I am not opposed to all divorces. Some marriages are empty. Some have suffered a total breakdown of trust. Others are like demolition derbies. None of them serve God. I am simply in favor of taking and keeping our vows—to the very best of our human ability—in all our relationships, in our work, and in the workplace. We need to be a people committed to keeping commitments.

Commitments Free Us

People tend to think of vows as confining, like chains or a locked door. Many of us approach vows as telling us what *not* to do or who we *can't* be. Vows are like cells.

They hold us back and in. They trap us. They eliminate our freedom. They kill the spirit.

The opposite is the case, at least from my perspective. Vows enable us to be fully free. In my marriage to Christine, I got to be myself. I could claim what I truly thought and felt. I shared my soul, my deepest wishes, my greatest fears, my anxieties and joys, and my worst and my best.

We are free to the degree we are aware. Our commitments enhance our awareness. Family and friends tell us who we are—the good, the bad, and, yes, the ugly. Those who know us best are able to shed light on our problems, issues, behaviors, and attitudes. They offer insight and revelations. They also inspire us and give us the needed kick in the butt or pat on the back.

Friendship is an institution. So is marriage and family, a church or synagogue, a school or club, or any true community. If they are functioning well, these institutions offer our lives a balance of dependence and independence. They provide roots and wings. They offer us the true freedom that is the result of being fully human. True institutions celebrate our humanity. They accept it, affirm it, and acknowledge it. In the hands of a healthy institution, we feel safe to be human.

Commitments Mature Us

Our culture encourages us to grow down and to be addicted to adolescence. We are told that if it feels good, do it. We are bombarded with the idea that breaking a commitment is no big deal. Life goes on. Kids adjust. Bull. Life goes on, but in a different direction. Kids adjust, and they are scarred. There is no more damaging experience in life than to be betrayed. There is no greater pain than to lose trust in somebody we love.

I see our culture as spoiled. We want what we want when we want it. We want it in a hurry. Yesterday. We want it easy. We want it hassle- and pain-free. We want it without much work. We want it because we have a right to it. Spoiled means rotten. When something rots, it fails to grow. It is decaying. It is no longer living.

Commitments make us mature. They make us grow. They keep us from living in denial, escaping, running away, or choosing the easy way out. Conflict is the context of creativity. Creativity is the fuel of maturation. Maturation and spirituality are one and the same.

Commitments keep us creating, moving forward, going deeper, becoming stronger, and developing courage. Commitments push us to build hope and find faith. Commitments truly are for adults only. We are our commitments. Our commitments declare who and what we are. They speak of our values and ethics. They make known our callings and faith. If we are committed to nothing, we are not yet an adult.

The Questions
To what am I committed? What vows have I failed to keep? Which vows can I say I have kept? To what must I become more deeply committed?

The Prayer
O God, make me true to my commitments. Give me the maturity to keep my vows. Let me be true to my word. Let me know the freedom and joy and satisfaction that can only be known by those mature enough to make a commitment. Amen.

Duty and Discipline

*The best discipline, maybe the only discipline
that really works, is self-discipline.*

—*Walter Kiechel III (in* Fortune)

There is a conviction. The evidence is in. The jury is no
longer out. The verdict is clear. We are convinced.

It is my conviction that all love requires a strong sense
of duty and discipline. Again, these are not popular
words within our culture. They are frowned upon. Duty
and discipline are thought of as negatives—no fun, joy-
less, a boring task, a meaningless chore. Life as an assem-
bly line on which we toil daily without thought or
emotional investment, the paycheck being the sole goal.

My son, Justin, is, without question, the great love of
my life. Being a good parent is my proudest achievement.
Parenting is loaded with duties, tasks, and chores of all
kinds: paying the bills, shopping for groceries, making
medical appointments, keeping the house and cars in
working order. But most important, parenting is being

available, a presence ready to listen, ready to talk, ready to share the burdens of his life.

In every loving relationship, there are mutual and fairly divided duties on both sides. These duties define the relationship. They declare what matters. If it is a duty, it means we feel it is essential. It must be done. It cannot be avoided. Something is accomplished which is of value.

Every loving relationship requires discipline. It is human nature to get lazy, to shirk a responsibility now and then, to forget what matters, or to take the road most traveled. The role of discipline is to remind us of what we want, to keep us focused on building even deeper and stronger bonds, and to make sure we do what is necessary to keep a relationship thriving.

The Duties of Love

The first duty of love is contact. I am amazed at the number of couples who come to me for counseling whose sole issue in the marriage is the absence of time. A marriage, a friendship, parenting, even my pastoral relationship to my congregation, all require time. Not just a little time, a lot of time. Not just quality time, but time, available time, time when we share our lives. Love requires being in touch and making connections.

It is easy to lose contact, to lose touch, to feel distant or detached. I know there are many relationships that can quickly reconnect or friendships that can take a year off and feel caught up in an hour. That is not the norm though. Most loving relationships require ample time. Time is like the safety net under the high wire of loving.

Taking time to be with those I love speaks of my love, expands it, and deepens it. I make good use of my time with those I love. I don't kill it, or buy it, or waste it. I make the most of that time.

The second duty of a loving relationship is talking, communicating by expressing our thoughts, feelings, and beliefs and exchanging glances and souls. Love must be expressed. It demands to be known. A good relationship works hard at this knowing: coming to understandings, acceptance, compromise, gaining insight, showing compassion. Love speaks. Love writes a story, a poem, with our lives.

The third duty of love is creating. Love must create or it will wither and die. It must create new things, new ideas, new hopes, new dreams, and new life. Love must expand. It must reach out and embrace life. An obsessive love, confined to just one person, a love that can think of nothing else but the beloved, is destined to suffocate. It's like placing a plastic bag over our heads. We cannot breathe for long. The view from inside the bag is totally distorted.

There are hundreds of duties to loving, maybe even thousands or more. These are the three I believe are most critical to establishing true bonds of love. What are your top three?

The Disciplines of Love

Discipline, more than duty, is an attitude. It is a way of thinking, a viewpoint. It is what we take seriously. It is making an investment of the whole person. To be disciplined means to be focused. It is a concentrated expression of what we value, what we cherish, what we love.

The first discipline of love is respect. It is a radical adherence to a belief in equality. It is the absence of game-playing. It is no competition. It is the genuine desire to share and to attain mutuality. Showing respect is believing that what someone else feels, thinks, and believes is every bit as important as your own. Putting respect into practice is difficult. It requires relinquishing control. It demands that we sacrifice some ego. It insists that we crawl inside someone's soul.

The second discipline of love is trust. Trust is a matter of faith. Faith is a work as well as a grace. The work of faith is worship. Worship is where we show what we believe. We name it. We claim it. We celebrate it.

Love is also a form of worship. We give thanks to the one we love. We confess and repent to the one we love. We offer our word. We speak the Gospel truth. We try to live our prayers with those we choose to love. Our worship speaks of our trust. It tells the story, the history, of our trust. It sings the praises of that trust.

Love has a third discipline that encases the first two: forgiveness. The art of forgiveness is a great discipline. Forgiveness enables love to survive, to be revived or restored, to deepen and grow, to be made holy. Forgiveness celebrates our humanity. It acknowledges we can fail. It affirms our vulnerability. It accepts the reality of disappointment and betrayal.

Jesus had 12 disciples, 12 men well trained in the disciplines of loving, 12 men who were tutored by a Master for 3 full years. These same men, when Jesus faced the death penalty, chose to betray him, deny him, doubt him, and go into hiding. Did Jesus stops loving them? No, not even Judas. His love for his disciples was grounded in grace.

Have you ever heard a carpenter or builder say, "Now this is a really well-built home"? You know exactly what they mean. They mean it was built with time and care, using the best materials and old-fashioned craftsmanship. This home was not whipped together overnight. This baby is solid as a rock.

A strong, loving relationship is a well-built home. Duty and discipline are the best materials available. They also provide the kind of craftsmanship that builds only the best.

The Questions

What do I consider the duties of love? What do I believe to be the disciplines required of love? Am I doing my duty? Am I well disciplined in my loving? How might I improve?

The Prayer

O God, let me do my duty. Let me love with discipline. Let me take time for those I love. Let me communicate my love in a million ways. Let my loving relationships create a hope-filled and happy life. Let my love declare my respect. Let me be one who is trusted. Let me be a forgiving soul. Let me be the presence of your grace in the lives of those I love. Amen.

Patience and Perseverance

Patience is bitter, but its fruit is sweet.
—Jean Jacques Rousseau

I was at home in Racine for a visit. I wanted to discuss my father's Alzheimer's with my mom and to see for myself what things were like. They were not good.

Dad searched my face for recognition. He would respond if I brought up Justin, my son and his only grandson, or Dad's childhood home in Cheshunt, England. He also liked hearing stories of when I was young, from our old neighborhood. I was never sure if he was familiar with what I was saying or if he simply enjoyed hearing a good story. His mind and memory were like Swiss cheese—the holes were expanding by the minute.

His diabetes was stable, but he had lost most feeling in his legs. He was fine with a walker, but he consistently forgot to use it. He fell often. He required stitches twice. My mother could not get him up, so she was forced to call for assistance. Once she had to call the ambulance; the other times she got family or neighbors to hoist him up.

Dad's appetite remained strong. He would flash his temper, then spend days begging Mom for forgiveness. His conversation was gibberish. It was like watching a television with the horizontal hold awry. He just flipped and flipped, over and over again, saying the same things and asking the same questions. It was a nightmare.

On the final night of my visit, he put his fist in my face and told me he knew what I was up to. I wanted to get rid of him. I wanted to interfere with his relationship with Mom. I was telling her lies. I didn't belong here. I kept telling him he was wrong. Ironically, on most counts, he was right.

The morning of my departure, the temperature had plummeted to below freezing, not that rare for late October in Wisconsin. I got up for my usual coffee time with Mom. Dad remained in bed for another hour, giving us our only true time to talk, to say what needed to be said, to feel free of my father's futile efforts to join the conversation.

However, this morning I could not find Mom. Dad was yelling for her, needing the assurance of her presence if he was to remain in darkness. Mom's being missing this early in the morning was odd. She would have told me if she were leaving. She would never leave Dad alone. I went outside. I called her name. There was no response. I went out back by the garage. I could hear her. She was sobbing. I found her sitting on the frozen cement in her nightgown. I brought her inside. Dad had remarkably poured coffee for the three of us. He called me by my name. He reprimanded Mom for being out in the cold. He did have some good mornings.

I told my mom that things would have to change, and soon. She told me that was her decision to make. I told her I was not going to lose her to Dad's disease. She told me it was her decision. I told her she was being unfair. She told me that life was unfair, and that when you love someone, you must be patient and persevere. She told me my generation did not understand that kind of loving. She called us the disposable generation. She was right.

I called her from the airport. I said to her, "Well, will you tell me when you cannot handle it anymore?" She promised she would. She apologized for scolding me. She knew I meant well. She reissued her admonition that I could take a few lessons from her on patience and perseverance. She said she felt much better after a good cry.

I told her I hated seeing her cry. She told me that's why they call it a *good* cry.

It would be another two years before Mom was ready to put Dad in a nursing home. She tenderly took care of him for a full seven years from the day of the Alzheimer's diagnosis. She was endlessly patient with him. Her love was consistent and seemingly infinite. Oh, yes, she had her days. She would yell at him. She would call and bitterly complain. But most of the time, she just kept loving her husband. She persevered in what she believed was her calling in life—until death us do part.

The Art of Hoping

Why did my mom put up with it? Why did she see her life become a jail cell filled with Alzheimer's? How could she not see that Dad belonged in a home? For a long time I did not understand. I do now.

Mom was waiting, patiently and with great perseverance. She was hoping for just a few more moments, a few more memories, a few more times when Dad would be with it, times when Dad would watch a whole television show with her or do the dishes or make a pot of coffee. She was wanting a few more times of Dad asking about his grandson or commenting on the beauty of snow, a few more times of feeling his arm on her shoulder and the warmth of his back against hers.

After seven years of waiting and collecting fragments, she gathered her memories up and let me place my father in a nursing home. She visited him there every day. She brought him a thermos of hot black coffee and his favorite windmill cookies. He was still her patient. She would continue to show him the love he deserved. Even when the day came that he knew her only as the lady with the cookies, she came. She lived her hope until the day he died. She kept her vow. Our vows keep track of our hopes.

The Questions
Am I patient? When? With whom? Why not? Do I persevere? Do I give love time to figure itself out? Have I walked away too soon? Have I waited too long? How will I know?

The Prayer
O God, I give great thanks for your patience. I am amazed at your perseverance. I am grateful you will not give up on me and that I am still a work in progress. I am the endless recipient of your grace. Amen.

Service and Sacrifice

In the old days, when things got rough, what
you did was without.

—Bill Copeland

I have worked with youth for 30 years, 25 of them as a youth minister. I have run playground programs and drop-in centers. I have taught confirmation classes and courses on everything from suicide to sex. I have led workshops and retreats. I have counseled individuals and groups. I have run spiritual support groups and dinner gatherings devoted to values clarification and ethical development.

When I work with adults interested in starting youth programs or ministries, I make sure there is ample time for questions. I listen carefully to what I am being asked. I learn a lot from the tone of a question. One of the first things I look for is what they are expecting from the experience. What is it that they hope to receive? What I tell them is this:

"If you are looking to adolescents to meet your needs, you are in the wrong line of work. Adolescents will have little to no interest in you. They will care about you but not often or for long. They may need you but will seldom show it, and they will never admit it. They will not be dependable. They will casually shirk a responsibility. They will be sarcastic and even mean. They will not be able to handle criticism.

"If you want to do youth ministry, you need to be well grounded. Centered. Meeting your emotional and spiritual needs elsewhere. Youth ministry is pure, unadulterated service. Guess who is the servant? Guess who is being served? You will be sacrificing your time, energy, sleep, heart, and often mind, and for what?

"For the chance to help a young person find his or her way in life. To create a few magical memories. To have some fun. To offer your presence and prayers and maybe a few words of wisdom. To let them know they matter. To listen and listen and listen. To encourage. To inspire. To be a chauffeur and chef. To let them know they are worth losing sleep over.

"Is this enough for you? Is this what you were looking for? Did you come here today to hear about service and sacrifice? Well, this is the truth. Youth ministry is all about service. The sacrifices are enormous. Burn-out is common. Frustration is the norm. Irritation is fundamental. But there is also a satisfaction so sweet and a sense of doing right, of being good, of following God. For some of you it will be enough."

Charity

If you read a King James Bible, in the famous 1 Corinthians, chapter 13, on love, you will see that the word for love is *charity*. In America, charity is thought of as pity. Charity is what the haves do for the have-nots. It is what winners offer losers. People like the idea of giving to a charity, but they hate the idea of needing to receive from a charity.

When charity is spoken of as love, as having the identical meaning, the whole idea of help shifts. Help becomes an expectation, something mutual. I will help you when you're in need. You will help me when I find myself in a tough spot. It is a reciprocal trade agreement, something people who love one another do automatically. With no questions asked, it is done.

Generosity

From the time when we're quite young, we are taught that it is blessed to give. We are encouraged to be generous. Morally, we are taught that we should give without expectation of anything in return. But we do, we do expect something: a thank you, a note, an acknowledgment of some kind. When we give a lot, we like a lot of credit. If we have made a sacrifice, we may even want it engraved on a plaque. There are few of us who give and expect nothing in return. We might do it occasionally but not frequently. If we do, we remember we did.

The genuinely generous person gives until it hurts. She gives away what she needs herself. She gives even when not to would make life easier for themselves. Generosity sacrifices. It does so because it believes it is called to serve. It gives more than it should, more than it can, more than can be repaid. It gives without thought but full of prayer.

God loves the cheerful giver, the person who is grateful to have the chance to give, to extend, to serve, to sacrifice, or even to hurt on someone's behalf. God's love is the prototype for generosity. It just flows and flows. It cannot stop giving. It cannot cease from offering everything it has. We are called to do likewise.

Our culture tells us to make good, sound investments. Have a thick wallet and a big bank account. Don't be a sucker. Give a little off the top. Play it safe. Think about the future. Will you be secure? It is good to be benevolent, but keep it under control. Make sure you get tax credit.

Our checkbooks say a great deal about our faith, and even more about our loving. Have we written a check recently that bore witness to our love of the outcast, the needy, the rejected of the world? Have we made any sacrifices on behalf of those who have little to nothing? We all think of ourselves as generous, but our checkbooks may tell another story.

Graciousness

The gracious host is someone who goes to great trouble to make guests feel welcome and at home. She cleans and decorates the house. She adds little touches to make the gathering special. She prepares the menu, paying attention to everyone's dietary needs and delights. She chooses the entertainment. She sets the table. She places the party favors. She attends every detail.

The gracious host greets his or her guests. The greeting is warm and full, and the guests know they are genuinely wanted. The host mingles, making sure conversation and beverages are flowing. If someone is being left out, he is quickly brought back in. The gracious host is working the party without letting anyone know she or he is working. It seems effortless, second nature. The gracious host makes everyone feel special. Everyone leaves happy and satisfied.

The Questions

Do I serve others? How? Willingly? What was the last genuine sacrifice I made? How did it make me feel? Why? How do I need to serve? What sacrifices do I need to make?

The Prayer

O God, keep me humble. Let me not be above serving others. Let me know the satisfaction of foot-washing. Let me make sacrifices that hurt, sacrifices that make me pay a spiritual price, the price of praise to the one true owner, the one and only giver of gifts, the one we call God. Amen.

Suffering and Loss

You don't have to suffer to be a poet.
Adolescence is enough suffering for anyone.
—John Ciardi

I presently have six young people, all friends of my son, all in their early 20s, living in my home. It is an experience. I am providing free room and board, providing each of them pursues his or her passion—writing, music, comic book art, animation, and/or schooling. It is a relaxed and enjoyable group of folks. The only hard part is planning a menu for a meal. Some are vegetarian. Several guests are vegan. Some could eat a cow in one sitting. All main meals resemble a smorgasbord.

I have learned a lot from living with this crew. I would rather take my appendix out with a shoehorn than listen to some of their music. Video games are addictive. Young people whisper really loud. Young people tend to drive loud cars. Young people think horror movies are funny. Young people are also good thinkers, emotionally sensitive, insightful, have wicked senses of humor, and are better able to live with one another than I would suspect most adults are. They form a community rather easily.

Living within this gathering has also reminded me of the central importance of love to human life. I have watched these young men and women fall in and out of love. I have observed their quest for love. I have witnessed their pain when a love ends. I have noted the reality of their suffering. I have paid close attention to their struggles: trying to communicate or compromise, trying to be understood or understand, trying to evict the games from the relationship, trying to be honest, trying to be mature.

Love is not easy. It is hard and often painful work. My heart aches when I see their heartbreak. I respect the agony of being betrayed by someone you love. I feel great empathy for those trapped in relationships they know are over, yet cannot bring themselves to leave. I know the difficulty of any good-bye. I am sensitive to the whole process of trying to figure out this thing called love.

I am amazed at the effort and energy love demands when you are young. And yet it is crucial to our whole spiritual maturation. Trust me, I have been impressed by many of their efforts; their displays of attention and affection; their romantic inclinations; their openness, frankness, and candor; and their desire for a healthy and happy relationship built on respect, trust, and strong communication. At times, I tease them that I feel like I am living on the set of a soap opera. They don't like hearing that. They find it condescending. They want my support. They want me to listen. They want me to offer wisdom when it is solicited. One of the most frequently asked questions is "Does it get any easier?" I calmly and serenely say "No. It gets even harder."

Pray for Strength

As we get older, we stop praying for an easy life and pray only to be stronger people. Our lives become more complex, more demanding, more stressful. We may not be dealing with peer pressure or the agony and ecstasy of falling in and out of love, but we are coping with the daily demands of the workplace, running a home, taking care of family and friends, and trying to serve our God. As we mature, our love expands. It grows deeper and wider.

Think of the love called for in Christian Scripture. The love of the outcast. The love of the leper. The love of the enemy. A love that is extravagant and endless in its mercy. A love that asks for nothing in return. A love that turns the other cheek. A love that washes feet, feeds

the hungry, clothes the naked, and frees the imprisoned.
A radical, reckless, and wild love. A love without bigotry
and without constraints. A volcanic love that flows and
flows.

As we spiritually mature, our loving requires greater
strength. We are called to love the tough to love. We are
commissioned to love even when we have no reason, no
desire, and no will to do so. We are asked to surrender
to a God who will do the loving for us. This, too, requires strength, a strong faith.

Pray for Healing

Love is littered with loss. The great challenge of love is
to endure the potential for its departure. All our love
lives have known their fair share of grief, broken hearts,
broken promises, broken dreams, tragic betrayals, and
disappointments of all kinds. All of our loves have expe-
rienced a breakdown of trust, a poverty of intimacy, an
empty shell of a relationship, divorce, death, departures
of myriad kinds.

When we lose a great love, we are shattered. Like
Humpty Dumpty, we are sure nothing and nobody can
put us back together again. But we can be put back
together. With time and tenderness and the real work of

grieving, we can be made whole. Our healing requires faith, a faith that forgives ourselves, a faith that forgives the one lost—for whatever the reason, a faith that forgives God for taking away. Our healing is the restoration of our faith in life, and our conviction that without loving, life is not worth the living.

Pray for Peace

Love is a battle: squabbles over control, incessant compromising, trying to make a point, hoping to be heard, trying to be fair. It is meeting a few needs of our own, staying loyal, keeping our vows and commitments, and being true, honest, and genuine. It is investing time and energy even when we are depleted. It is praying that when war breaks out, we will find a way to make peace.

Love is art. It is discipline. It is work. It will require some suffering. It will certainly know loss and defeat. Love is held together by the glue of peacemaking: settling problems, resolving issues, taking stands, giving in, finding common ground, picking our battles, letting go and letting God, surrendering our battles to a Higher Power.

Peace is always in search of makers, especially in love. Who will take the first step? Who will say "I'm sorry"? Who will ask to be forgiven or for a fresh start? Who will just drop it? Who will let it rest? Who will be wise enough to think "This, too, shall pass"? Peacemaking is the foundation upon which true love is built.

There are so many warring couples out there and so few cease-fires and so little compromise. Peace is seldom pursued or made. Time is not being taken. Talk is not happening. Forgiveness is never offered. There is no prayer, no Higher Power, no faith in love.

The same is true among nations. We are suffering from a lack of love, a lack of doing the hard work of love, a lack of forgiveness, a lack of mercy. We endure a lack of listening, a lack of talking, a lack of respect and trust, and a lot of squabbling, name-calling, acts of violence, and words of hate.

Americans must learn to love Arabs. After September 11, that is tough. We want to scapegoat Arabs. We want someone to blame. We want an enemy. We want to defeat someone and to lift up ourselves. True peace, however, will be made from understanding and mutual respect. It will come out of the grueling work of finding common ground, before there is any ground at all.

Love, true love, spiritual love, sacrificial love, the love depicted in Christian, Jewish, Muslim, and other

Scripture, is a love willing to suffer on behalf of peace. It is a love that will accept losses as the price to be paid for a lasting peace. It is a deep and abiding and divine love. It is the very nature of God.

The Questions

Why must we suffer? What are the lessons my losses have taught me? How can I be a peacemaker? When? Where? With whom? Why or why not? How can I strengthen my loving?

The Prayer

O God, grant me a faith that is willing to suffer. Let me listen to my losses. Let me learn from them. Let me squeeze love out of the pain. Let me know that love asks all of me. All I have. All I am. All I can or will be. Love demands my best. O God, you are the author of all love. Let me absorb the perfection of your love. Let me funnel that love on a waiting world. Let me make peace in all I say and do. Amen.

Above and Beyond

Nobody has ever measured, even the poets,
how much a heart can hold.

—*Zelda Fitzgerald*

Her walks were a daily ritual. I saw her on several occasions. We never spoke, but we would nod hello. In every kind of weather, whether the wilting heat of August or the piercing cold of January, she would be pushing that buggy. Inside was a small boy, I think, by now, almost five. He was always wrapped in blankets, though fewer in the summer, the plastic breathing tube protruding and the baseball hat and thick glasses barely visible.

He had been permanently injured in a pool accident at the age of two. He had nearly drowned, been revived, but now had minimal function. A once bright, smiling, and scooting around little boy, he was now a blank face, guttural sounds, and spastic movements in the arms and legs.

She was his grandmother. She must have been in her late 70s, thick of bust and middle, wearing big sneakers, an apron, and lots of rouge, with her hair up in curlers and covered in a colorful kerchief.

It was a beautiful day. Pure spring. Soft, powdery blue sky. Wisps of cloud. A light summery breeze. The air fragrant with lilacs. The sun gentle. I saw her coming. I considered crossing the street. The sight of the buggy made me queasy. I would avert my eyes, as if a monster lay inside, or worse, a badly damaged little boy without hope for the future. As we neared one another, she spoke, "Is this the most lovely day, or what?"

"It is truly spectacular!" I said with as much enthusiasm as I could feign.

"I have been telling Todd all about it. Letting him know the colors of the tulips and which birds I have spotted. He loves hearing the birds. I know when he gets excited. His head rocks. Spring is his favorite season. Isn't it Todd?"

I looked. There in the buggy was a little boy with beautiful big blue eyes. His Atlanta Braves baseball hat was rocking back and forth. He had a sliver of a smile. I said hello. He grunted and kicked.

"Thank you," she said. "Most folks won't even look. He is still my boy. I'm sure you know the story of his injuries. Everyone in town does. He has had it tough. Poor thing. But he loves these rides. I know he does. Everyone tells me I am kidding myself, or that I am nuts, but I know better. I know he loves being outside, plus I always tell him that God is helping me push the buggy."

"You are a remarkable woman," I said with wet eyes.

"Oh no, Todd is remarkable, and so is God. I have finally stopped and smelled the roses, all because of Todd. I know every inch of this town and how it looks in every season. God has taught me to notice the beauty of details. God has given me Todd to teach. I always wanted to be a teacher, but I didn't have the brains or the bucks. Now I am. I am Todd's teacher.

"You have a wonderful day. Todd and I are going to watch the seagulls float on the wind at the beach. Aren't we Todd?!"

She walked off smiling, Todd grunting and rocking his head. I was dumbstruck. Where on earth does that kind of love come from? How could she do it day after day after day? Did Todd even know? Was his head always rocking? I shook my head and thought out loud, "That kind of love comes from above."

A woman. A walk. A damaged child. A parable. A lesson of love. A love that went way above and beyond the world's expectations. Above and beyond and into a territory we call heaven. Eternity. A place where great sacrificial love is no longer a mystery, not even a miracle, but the norm.

Love Is Always in the Red

Great love has a great cost. It requires a huge investment of time and energy, patience and perseverance, mercy, trust, respect, hope, and faith. It is a love that must be willing to sacrifice, serve, even suffer. It is a love that does not keep score. It does not ask to be paid. It is happy being in the red.

What is a great love? A great love is a love that reveals the love of God. It is a love that speaks God's name. It is a love that makes known the Grace of God.

A great love takes our breath away. It gives us a lump in our throat and a shiver up and down our spine, and leaves us dumbstruck. We are not left stupid by the sight of a great love. We are simply silent because we know this love speaks the Word of God. This is a love that tells a story, a sacred story, a gospel, the truth.

Love Demands the Impossible

The world has grown cynical about love. It has cheapened it, candy-coated it, and made it into some sappy sentimental sitcom mess.

The world has an attitude about love. Love has questionable motivations and few morals. Love plays endless games. It is self-seeking and mostly about the pursuit of pleasure. Love is what we call lust when lust doesn't get its way.

The world has low expectations of love. If the going gets tough, love is gone. If you get bored, trade it in for a newer model. Love should be spontaneous, easy, and little work; if it is not, move on. There are always more fish in the sea.

A great love has a totally different perspective. A great love follows a path that leads to the Kingdom of God. A great love rejects the ways of the world. A great love expects and gets the impossible.

A great love is a miracle. It is a hope against hope. It is wishful thinking. It is a leap of faith. It makes no sense. It is illogical. It has no rewards other than the giving of it. It is the belief that with God all things are possible.

A great love does not try to explain itself or to offer a proof or a defense. It just offers evidence. It is a star witness. It gives testimony to the power of love to heal and transform. As Jesus taught, there is no greater love than to lay down your life for your friends. That is a love the world cannot understand. It can only be comprehended by the mind of faith.

The Questions
What is the greatest love I have known? What is the greatest act of love I have witnessed? What would it mean to me to live without fear?

The Prayer
O God, let me know a great love. Let me be a source of great love. Let me claim the greatness of your grace. Let me go above and beyond the world's call to take care of only myself and have the strength of faith to seek to care for the whole world. Amen.

Afterword

I am a minister. I have been for 25 years. In that quarter of a century, I have sat on many deathbeds. I have held hands and prayed. I have listened to final words, words spoken with tears of joy and sorrow, with expressions of gratitude and regret. Simple statements of great poignancy. From folks aged 10 to nearing 100, I have been the honored recipient of their wisdom.

These closing comments have taught me a great deal—not all that much about dying, but a ton about living. About what matters, what counts, what makes a lasting impression, and what makes a difference. I have been dumbstruck at the consistency of these commentaries, how they echo one another, how they state and restate the same themes, and how similar are the priorities they declare.

Let me be clear on this. I have never heard one person on his or her deathbed say anything remotely like "I wish I had more time to make more money," "I wish I had more time to work," or "I wish I had bought that Porsche."

The sentiments folks choose to express in their last days are focused on one thing and one thing only—*love*. Love is at the core of every sacred commentary I have ever heard. Love is the final legacy left in words.

As a person's life is winding down, it would appear that everything begins to shrink and focus. The energy depletes. The words are slow and quiet. But the power is enormous. The subject matter always the same. The desire to have spent more time with loved ones. The wish to forgive or be forgiven. The regret of having hurt someone. The joy of having shared a life with a soul mate. The longing for one more day of health and happiness, to be spent doing the simplest things with one or more of one's cherished friends or family.

On a deathbed, as life fades like a sunset, we humans rejoice in our loves and reclaim our need to love some more. It is just that simple. Just that clear.

Love is a work as well as a grace. It is an art. It is an education that lasts a lifetime. It is an adventure. It is a beautifier. It takes place in the mundane but is jammed with miracles. Love is always in style. It is the fruit of every season.

It is my hope that this little book has shed some light on the matter of love. This is not easy to do. Love is the source of all light. Trying to shed light on the source of light is like trying to chew our teeth. Still, try we must. The subject is sacred. The topic of ultimate concern. The need to understand is overwhelming. If I have enabled you to take some time to reflect on the essential nature of love, the hard spiritual work it demands, the eternal rewards it has to offer, then I will have succeeded.

I know for certain, this little book was written with all the love I could muster.